THE NEXT STAGE OF

CATHOLIC RELIGIOUS LIFE

Postmodern Lay
Mystical-Prophetic Intentional Communities
Based on Ecological Spirituality

JOE HOLLAND

www.joe-holland.net

PACEM IN TERRIS PRESS

Devoted to the radical-traditional vision of Saint John XXIII,
prophetic founder of Postmodern Global Catholic Social Teaching,
and to the search for a Postmodern Global Humanistic-Ecological Civilization,
which will draw on the spiritual wisdom-traditions of Christianity
and on all the spiritual wisdom-traditions of our human family.

www.paceminterrispress.com

*Pacem in Terris Press publishes scholarly books directly or indirectly related to
Catholic Social Teaching and its commitment to justice, peace, ecology,
and spirituality, and on behalf of the search for a Postmodern Ecological Civilization.*

*In addition, in order to support ecumenical and interfaith dialogue, as well as dialogue with
other spiritual seekers, Pacem in Terris Press publishes scholarly books from other Christian
perspectives, from other religious perspectives, and from perspectives
of other spiritual seekers that promote justice, peace, ecology,
and spirituality for our global human family.*

*Opinions or claims expressed in publications from Pacem in Terris Press
represent the opinions and claims of the authors and do not necessarily represent
the official position of Pacem in Terris Press, the Pacem in Terris Ecological Initiative,
Pax Romana / Catholic Movement for Intellectual & Cultural Affairs - USA
or its officers, directors, members, and staff.*

PACEM IN TERRIS PRESS
is the publishing service of

PAX ROMANA
CATHOLIC MOVEMENT FOR INTELLECTUAL & CULTURAL AFFAIRS
USA
*1025 Connecticut Avenue NW, Suite 1000,
Washington DC 20036
www.paceminterris.net*

This book is dedicated to my cousin,
Sister Mary Isidore Lennon, RSM (1901-1986),
of the Sisters of Mercy in the Saint Louis area,
devoted lover and servant of the poor and the sick;

And to my many and dear friends in the Maryknoll family
of brothers, lay members, priests, and sisters,
for their heroic and holy dedication to the Gospel of Jesus the Christ,
in service of global mercy, justice, peace, ecology, truth, and love;

And to the memory of Sister Margaret Clare Dreckman, OSF (1917-2006),
past leader of the Sisters of Saint Francis of Dubuque, Iowa,
long filled with the charismatic power of the Holy Spirit,
wise spiritual counselor to me and to so many others,
and dear friend;

And to the memory of Venerable Solanus Casey, OFM Cap. (1870-1957),
member of the Capuchin branch of the followers of St. Francis of Assisi,
lover of the poor and the sick,
and Spirit-filled instrument of God's healing power.

Those who live on the land can hardly fail to appreciate the
nobility of the work they are called upon to do.
They are living in close harmony with Nature – the majestic temple of Creation.
Their work has to do with the life of plants and animals,
a life that is inexhaustible in its expression,
inflexible in its laws, rich in allusions to
God the Creator and Provider.

SAINT JOHN XXIII
MATER ET MAGISTRA

An ecological spirituality ... can motivate us to
a more passionate concern for the protection of our world ...
The ecological crisis is also a summons to profound interior conversion ...
What [we] need is an "ecological conversion"...
a loving awareness that we are not disconnected from the rest of creatures,
but joined in a splendid universal communion ...
[with] awareness that each creature reflects something of God
and has a message to convey to us.

FRANCIS OF ROME
CARE FOR OUR COMMON HOME

TABLE OF CONTENTS

1

INTRODUCTION

I N 2015, POPE FRANCIS (elected as Bishop of Rome in 2013) issued his great 2015 ecological encyclical, LAUDATO SI' - *On Care for
Our Common Home.*[1] Francis' encyclical addresses what he calls "integral ecology," which means holistic ecology. With that concept, Francis integrates concern for natural ecology with concern for human
ecology, and especially in relation to humans who are poor or in any
way vulnerable. At the same time, he links his integrated concepts of
human ecology and natural ecology with his call for "*ecological spirituality*," which we might also describe as mystical-prophetic "spiritual
ecology."

New Stage of Catholic Spirituality

In this book, I propose further integrating Francis' concept of "integral ecology" – again, including natural ecology and human ecology
– with a rephrasing of his concept of "ecological spirituality" as "spiritual ecology." I propose integrating those three concepts into a single
framework that I call the "*creative communion of life*," or alternately
"*ecological co-creativity*."[2]

---

[1] For the Vatican's official English text of this encyclical letter, see:
*http://w2.vatican.va/content/francesco/en/encyclicals/documents/papa-francesco_20150524_
enciclica-laudato-si.html.*

[2] For an initial exploration of the creative communion of life, see my earlier book,
CREATIVE COMMUNION: *Toward a Spirituality of Work* (Paulist Press, 1989).

Within this comprehensive framework, I also propose that we understand all cosmic creation, which we now know is evolving, as analogously alive. This proposed comprehensive framework understands all of cosmic creation as both holistic and evolving, and as embracing *the interwoven natural, human, and spiritual fabric of life's integral ecology,* across our loving Creator's beloved garden-planet Earth.

Further, I propose that this new ecological spirituality (spiritual ecology) represents a new historical development in Catholic spirituality, in Christian spirituality more broadly, and even in human spirituality. Within that framework, I also propose that the emergence of this new spirituality in Catholic form requires a new stage in what has been called "religious life," although in my analysis it will be given a different name.

This book is largely excerpted, and further developed, from my earlier and more complex book POSTMODERN ECOLOGICAL SPIRITUALITY,[3] and it is directed to a more narrow but important audience, namely Catholic intentional communities of "religious life," and especially in the United States. I offer it as a reflection piece that may be of some use in exploring the new stage of ecological spirituality, and also in helping some contemporary Catholic communities of "religious life" to sponsor experiments in new lay communities based on ecological spirituality, and to begin to transform their entire institution.

Postmodern Transformation of
Civilization & Spirituality

In this book, and in my other writings, the term "postmodern" is not used in the common and nihilist sense of what I have called "Academic Postmodernism." From my viewpoint, Academic Postmodern-

---

[3] The full title is POSTMODERN ECOLOGICAL SPIRITUALITY: *Catholic-Christian Hope for the Dawn of a Postmodern Ecological Civilization Rising from within the Spiritual Dark Night of Modern Industrial Civilization* (Pacem in Terris Press, 2017).

ism is not truly postmodern but *only late modern.* By contrast, the word "postmodern," as used here, means *ecologically regenerative beyond the Modern Era.* It also refers to what I have named the seminally emerging "Postmodern Ecological Civilization."

Also in my view, o Modern Industrial Civilization (1500 to 2000 CE) is now breaking down, especially ecologically but also socially and spiritually. Correlative with that breakdown is a decline of the modern form of spirituality, which I describe as *psychological* – in contrast to postmodern spirituality which, again, I see as *ecological.* The following chart gives a simplistic outline for this current and correlative transformation of civilization and spirituality.

CORRELATIVE TRANSFORMATIONS

ERA:	MODERN	POSTMODERN
CIVILIZATION:	MODERN INDUSTRIAL CIVILIZATION	POSTMODERN ECOLOGICAL CIVILIZATION
SPIRITUALITY:	MODERN PSYCHOLOGICAL SPIRITUALITY *(Interiority)*	POSTMODERN ECOLOGICAL SPIRITUALITY *(Co-Creativity)*

Hope & Prayer

In conclusion, I hope and pray that this book, inspired by Francis' prophetic encyclical LAUDATO SI', may prove of some small service in promoting the ecological spirituality that Pope Francis Rome has called for. I further hope and pray that this book may advance Francis' prophetic postmodern global call for the integral-ecological regeneration of life across our loving Creator's beloved garden-planet Earth.

2

PAST LONG WAVES OF

CATHOLIC SPIRITUAL ENERGY

T his lengthy chapter reviews the past five historical long waves of what I call *"Catholic mystical-prophetic intentional communities."*[1] Those past long waves flow from the foundational lay roots of the early church up to the modern Western "apostolic" form of "religious life," which is now experiencing late modern decline within the 'advanced' industrialized countries. This most recent last long wave of modern "apostolic-religious" communities is now yielding to the emerging postmodern wave of new lay eco-spiritual movements.

Co-Creative Role of Catholic
Mystical-Prophetic Intentional Communities

Catholic mystical-prophetic intentional communities are intense centers of spiritual energy, with historically evolving institutional expressions in long waves of Catholic spirituality. Each wave arises as a strategic-spiritual response to a new wave of civilization. Again, within the present postmodern transition, the modern wave of "apostolic religious life" is in decline. At the same time, there is emerging

---

[1] I have for the most part rounded off dating of the beginning and ending of the dominance of each post-apostolic wave to the nearest hundredth year. Of course, the emergence and decline of the past forms overlap across long historical periods. For the beginning of Christianity, I have chosen as the rounded-off date the year 30.

an early postmodern wave of a fresh lay form of Catholic mystical-prophetic intentional communities. This book sees these new lay movements as called, in partnership with traditional forms of "religious life," to promote a Catholic form of Postmodern Ecological Spirituality on behalf of global regeneration of life's integral ecology.

"Religious life" is an ancient and rich tradition in Catholic Christianity, with its modern "apostolic" form being one of many forms in its evolutionary history. Further, since a new form is now emerging and its identity is lay, this new lay form requires that we examine critically the cosmologically dualist character of the concept "religious life."

Beyond "Religious" Dualism

Since the emerging postmodern form of Catholic spiritual energy is taking a distinctly lay form, and since the dualistic phrase "religious life" is not of evangelical origin, I prefer to describe all such spiritual communities in this still evolving tradition by the broader name of Catholic mystical-prophetic intentional communities.

Although some prefer the phrase "vowed life" or "consecrated life" over "religious life," those alternatives also do not seem adequate. All Christians have a vowed and consecrated life in the sacraments of Baptism (baptismal vows) and Confirmation (consecration with oil). Further, Catholic married couples have a vowed life in the sacrament of Marriage (marriage vows). In addition, while the "religious vows" of poverty, chastity, and obedience constitute an important form of "vowed life," they do not constitute a Catholic sacrament, as do baptismal and marriage vows and the consecration of Confirmation.

Again and for those reasons, this book uses the non-dualist phrase of Catholic mystical-prophetic intentional communities. The core institutional identity of such communities has been, throughout their evolution, *their intense personal and institutional commitment to the mystical and prophetic dimensions of Christian discipleship.*

10

As mentioned, however, the Western Catholic spiritual tradition is partly problematic, because its classical cosmological dualism of *'higher'* ("religious") and *'lower'* ("secular") "states of life" came not from Jesus' original lay movement, but from the Neo-Platonist tradition, parts of which both classical and modern forms of Western Catholic Ascetical Theology incorporated. By contrast, in Jesus' teaching, as is clear in the New Testament, spirituality is not a "state in life" but rather it is a "way of life," and there is only one foundational way of Christian discipleship, namely, *the lay baptismal "Way" of Jesus' own lay mystical-prophetic path.*

Special Historical Roles

Catholic Christianity is heir to a long series of distinctive and creative movements of special mystical-prophetic intentional communities. Those movements have emerged historically in strategic spiritual response to profound historical transformations within the contextual civilization.

Those creative spiritual movements have included, for example, Desert Fathers and Desert Mothers, Irish-Keltic monasticism and Latin Benedictine Monasticism, Augustinians who began as medieval canons, medieval mendicant Franciscans and Dominicans, late medieval Beguines and Beghards, and modern apostolic communities like Jesuits, Daughters of Charity, Religious of the Sacred Heart, Sisters of Mercy, etc. Such women's and men's communities have long been the Holy Spirit's special instruments for renewing both church and society, albeit always in a limited and imperfect manner.

Catholic "religious communities" have played significant roles by providing important gifts for renewing and sustaining the vocation, communion, and mission of all Jesus' disciples throughout the wider church. In these "religious communities," some of Jesus' lay disciples have gathered together to live Jesus' call in a more intense way as a

11

renewing service to the wider community of all Jesus' disciples, as well as to the entire human family, and even to all of creation.

Yet we need to remember that the purpose of these *special* Catholic mystical-prophetic communities is part of the wider purpose of the *general* mystical-prophetic community of all Jesus' disciples. We need also to recall that the wider and full community of Jesus' disciples, which we call "church," exists for one central purpose, namely, *to serve as the evangelical-sacramental instrument of the Holy Spirit's healing and deeper sanctification of our wounded creation and of our wounded human family within it.*

Human sin has wounded and continues to wound the Creator's beloved creation and humanity within it. The Holy Spirit's healing and deeper sanctification of all creation and of humanity within it, through the "Way" of Jesus, comes to partial fulfillment when Christians gather in love as the imperfect community of disciples that we call "church."

Further, it is the evangelical-sacramental *lay mission* of all Jesus' disciples to carry the "good news" of that healing and deeper sanctification to all peoples. Those of us who are Jesus' disciples witness to the reality of that healing and deeper sanctification by loving communion within our community of disciples, as well as with all our human sisters and brothers across planet Earth. We also witness to it by our loving communion with all our loving Creator's beloved other creatures across our garden-planet Earth and throughout the Cosmos. For Christians, this healing sanctification partly takes place now, but its full power will be revealed only in the *Eschaton.*

Again, within this historical framework, what may now be called *special* Catholic mystical-prophetic communities have the special historical vocation of reforming and deepening the identity and mission of the *general* mystical-prophetic community of "Church."

SIX HISTORICAL LONG WAVES

OF CATHOLIC SPIRITUAL ENERGY

HISTORICAL CONTEXT	HISTORICAL FORM	HISTORICAL MISSION
Cities of Oppressive & Idolatrous Roman Empire	FOUNDATIONAL LAY COMMUNITIES *(30-300)*	Live as Messianic Community often under Roman Imperial Persecution
Cities of Christianized Roman Empire	CLASSICAL COENOBITICAL COMMUNITIES *(Desert Hermits)* *(300-500)*	Ascetical Flight to Rural Wilderness as Counter-point to Urban "Clergy's" Imperial Church
Rural Feudalism after Fall of Western Roman Empire	FEUDAL MONASTIC COMMUNITIES *(500-1200)*	Evangelize Migrating 'Barbarian' Tribes & with Them Rebuild Western Christian Civilization
Late Medieval Bourgeois Commercial City-States as Seeds of Modern Capitalism	MEDIEVAL MENDICANT COMMUNITIES *(1200-1500)*	Evangelize New Bourgeois Culture & Challenge its Foundational Temptations *(Defense of Poor, Ecology, & Democracy)*
Modern Western Bourgeois Industrial-Colonial Nation-States *(Initially Liberal-Capitalist & later also Scientific-Socialist)*	MODERN APOSTOLIC COMMUNITIES *(1500-2000)*	Apostolates of Health, Education, & Welfare, especially for Urban Working Class, Poor Rural Areas, & Colonized Peoples
Breakdown of Modern Western Industrial-Colonial Civilization & Emergence of Postmodern Global Electronic-Ecological Civilization	POSTMODERN LAY ECOLOGICAL COMMUNITIES *(2000 ...)*	Overcome Late Modern Western Culture of Death & Seek Global Regeneration of Life's Evolving Ecology across its Interwoven Natural, Human, & Spiritual Fabric

Simplifying the complexity of this still developing tradition into what the great German sociologist Max Weber called "ideal types," we may identify within the evolving history of Catholic mystical-prophetic intentional communities the following six successive long waves (summarized in the chart on the preceding page).[2] For the most part, the dating of these waves is rounded off here to the nearest hundredth year. These six long waves may be described as follows.

- *Foundational Lay Communities* (30-300) of the early church, including women and men, married and singles, and families with children – witnessing to Jesus' messianic vision under the oppression and persecution of the unjust and idolatrous Roman Empire;

- *Classical Coenobitical Communities* (300-500) of "Desert Mothers" and "Desert Fathers," who moved to remote rural areas

---

[2] For the history of "religious life," I am especially endebted to: Lawrence Catta, Raymond Fitz, Gertrude Foley, Thomas Giordino & Carol Lynchburg SHAPING THE COMING AGE OF RELIGIOUS LIFE (Seabury Press, 1985); Institute for Research, NEW BEGINNINGS, RELIGIOUS LIFE EVOLVES (Lumen Vitae, 1983); Gerald Arbuckle, STRATEGIES FOR GROWTH IN RELIGIOUS LIFE (ALBA HOUSE, 1987) OUT OF CHAOS: *Refounding Religious Congregations* (Paulist Press, 1988); Lori Felknor CRISIS IN RELIGIOUS VOCATION (Paulist Press, 1989); Mary Jo Leddy, "Beyond the Liberal Model of Religious Life," THE WAY (Summer, 1989.

Since the time when the above-noted books were published, much more has been written about the history of "religious life," including about refounding, though the majority have been from perspectives internal to "religious life." Among these books is Diarmuid O'Murchu's magisterial text, RELIGIOUS LIFE IN THE 21ST CENTURY: THE PROSPECT OF REFOUNDING (Orbis Books, 2016). That book does a masterful job of synthesizing recent explorations on the history and present crisis of modern "religious life." It also provides a prophetic vision and process for discernment about possible "refounding" with "religious communities."

Note that this list of six leaves out some additional models – for example, medieval "canons" as well as the Beguines and Beghards, since such additional models, while important and creative, never became pervasive. Also, this listing does not agree with the distinction sometimes made between earlier modern "apostolic" communities and later modern "missionary" communities. For this listing, both fall under the "apostolic" model.

beyond the urban-centered Empire and outside the ecclesial framework of the new Imperial Church with its now hierarchical urban "clergy," who as religious legitimizers of the Empire often tended to change the Evangelical message of the Cross to an imperial military symbol;

- *Feudal Monastic Communities* (500-1200) which, after the fall of the Western Roman Empire, lived within rural Feudalism to evangelize the conquering 'barbarian' German tribes, and with them to regenerate Western Civilization by creating intellectual-spiritual centers and communitarian-agrarian foundations, many of which would later become medieval towns and modern cities (for example, the city of Vienna, developed by Irish-Keltic monks).

- *Medieval Mendicant Communities* (1200-1500), which challenged the early bourgeois temptations of the new urban culture of the high Middle Ages, and reached out especially to youth in the medieval university towns – themselves expanding from the new commercial wealth generated from the Eastern "Silk Roads" that were re-opened as trading routes by the West's violent military "Crusades;"[3]

- *Modern Apostolic Communities* (1500-2000), which ministered within the 'advanced' bourgeois civilization that was becoming Modern Western Industrial-Colonial Capitalism, and did so by providing professional "apostolates" especially to the industrial urban working class and to poor rural farming families, as well as to conquered and colonized peoples, primarily by pioneering and developing modern social-welfare institutions for education, health-care, and other charitable services;

---

[3] As noted earlier, in the High Middle Ages, there emerged many military forms of monasticism – a development far from Jesus' non-violent message. Again, see Rodriguez-Picavea, LOS MONJES GUERREROS.

- *Projected Postmodern Lay Ecological Communities* (2,000 …), which is seen here as called to become grounded in the emerging Postmodern Ecological Spirituality, to promote a future Postmodern Ecological Civilization, and to plant seeds for the postmodern global regeneration of life's integral ecology, especially on behalf of vulnerable humans and all other threatened living creatures across our loving Creator's beloved garden planet Earth.

Again, against the background of this historical unfolding, this book sees the new lay ecological wave as called to celebrate the creative communion of life's integral ecology, throughout its interwoven natural, human, and spiritual fabric. But let us now review the past five long waves, including the now declining "apostolic-religious" wave.

Foundational Lay Communities
Witnessing within the Roman Empire
(30-300)

The first wave of Catholic mystical-prophetic intentional communities is the *foundational lay period* of Christianity during its first three centuries – originally Jewish but quickly expanding into Arabian and African Christianity, as well as into Greco-Roman and Keltic Christianity, and into the Christianity of Persia, India, and perhaps even China. Within the territories of the Roman Empire, the identity and mission of the early and foundational lay communities carried a *messianic rejection of the Empire's idolatry and injustice.*

"Way" of Jesus as Lay

The brutal Roman Empire had crucified Jesus, a Jewish lay teacher ("rabbi"), as a political threat. The Empire also subsequently executed Peter and Paul, both Jewish laypersons, as well as thousands of other Christians, all of whom were lay. That foundational period has been called the "Age of Martyrs," since the Empire executed so many Christians for following the "Way" of Jesus.

In all the regions of this first wave, throughout the apostolic church and for several centuries after, Christianity was *exclusively lay*. In that first wave, there was no such thing as the "religious state in life" (with "state" meaning status or class), nor was there any such thing as the "clerical state in life." Over time, there emerged, of course, disciples who were ordained for authority-bearing offices (deacons, presbyters, and bishops), as well as disciples with special charisms for the community, including communities of virgins and widows. Yet all were lay.

Again, in the church's early centuries, these offices and charisms did not represent separate "states-in-life" (to use the language of the contemporary Canon Law of the Western or Roman Catholic Church). There was originally *only the one lay "way" of the baptized,* including ordained lay leaders and lay disciples with special charisms. There was only the New Testament's "Way" of Jesus.

The word "lay" comes from the Greek word *Laos,* which means "people." In the Greek Septuagint translation of the Hebrew Scriptures and in Greek texts of the New Testament, *Laos* means the holy, royal, priestly People of God. Further, in the New Testament the Greek work *kleros* (from which we get "clergy") means "chosen." The New Testament uses the word *kleros* to signify that everyone within the *Laos* of Jesus' disciples is "chosen."

Thus, neither the "religious state" nor the "clerical state" is a constitutive dimension of the Church, for they did not exist in the early centuries of Christianity. Further, the Catholic tradition came to understand Baptism, Confirmation, Ordination, and Marriage as "sacraments." But the canonical "clerical and religious states" are not sacraments. Even so, both often became elevated in practice above the "laity," and thus above the sacraments of Baptism, Confirmation, and Marriage.

Nonetheless, the "religious and clerical states in life" represented creative legal-cultural additions to the late classical form of Catholic Christianity, and they later carried over into medieval modern forms. Yet, again, those adaptations were not part of the church's apostolic foundation.

End of Persecuted Lay Church
& Rise of Imperial Hierarchical Church

Toward the end of the foundational period, Roman imperial leaders saw the lay movement of Christianity – despite persecution, spreading rapidly and broadly throughout the Empire – as offering the possibility of holding together the externally threatened and internally disintegrating imperial society.

As external attacks by migrating 'barbarian' German tribes intensified, and as the Empire began to degenerate internally, the Christian movement appeared to imperial leaders to offer renewed and unifying organizational strength. That was because the Christian cosmopolitan vision was not limited to a specific geographic, ethnic, or class identity.

From the time of the fifty-seventh Roman Emperor Constantine the Great (272-337), ruling from Constantinople (formerly Byzantium) in what is today's Turkey, the imperial government constructed an ecclesial-political alliance with the Catholic bishops of the imperial regions (called "dioceses"). The Roman Empire, which had crucified Jesus and probably thousands of his followers, appealed to the episcopal leaders of Jesus' disciples in the desperate hope of saving itself. Most Catholic bishops accepted the opportunity, though the Coptic church of Africa resisted imperial take-over and continued to suffer persecution from the Imperial State in its new partnership with the Imperial Church.

18

That Catholic acceptance eventually led to Christianity becoming the official religion of the Empire, reshaped by imperial consciousness and backed by the coercive power of the Imperial State. Within that profound political shift, the first history of the Catholic Church, written by the Catholic bishop Eusebius of Caesarea (c. 263-339) who was close to the imperial household, described the Emperor Constantine ruling on his throne as reflecting an *imperial image of God*.[4]

That imperial image, Christianized as "*Christ the King*," would dominate Catholic Christianity until modern times when first African-American and later Latin-American Liberation Theology recovered, for both Catholicism and Protestantism, the alternative prophetic biblical image of Jesus as proclaimed in Luke 4:18-19. That is the image of *Jesus the Liberator*, recalling not David the King but Moses the Prophet. The following lengthy quotation may be helpful for understanding how profound is that symbolic shift in Christian Soteriology.

> *In the impending collapse of Western political-economic and ecclesial-spiritual hegemony, we are now experiencing a paradigm-shift in the foundational biblical metaphor for evangelization from David to Moses, or from the Temple at Zion to the Covenant at Shechem. Since the time of Constantine, Western Catholic Christianity pursued evangelization under the symbolic image of "Yeshua Ha-Mashiach" (Jesus the Christ, or Joshua the Messiah), understood hierarchically and triumphally as Christ the King.*

> *That foundational Davidic or Zionist image understands the Word of God as coming in priestly manner to the people through the established social structures (equivalent of the king), with the established social order presumably reflecting the Divine order.*

---

[4] See EUSEBIUS: THE CHURCH HISTORY, transl. Paul L. Maier (Kraeger, 2007). Note that, contrary to GENESIS 1:27, the image does not include woman.

Today, however, with Western de-Christianization, with the post-colonial emancipation of the formerly colonized peoples of the Global South, and with the threatened ecological destruction of at least half of the Creator's beloved species on planet Earth, the foundational biblical metaphor of evangelization is shifting.

It is now swinging to the other biblical pole of the counter-cultural symbol of "Yeshua Ha-Mashiach," that is, Jesus (or Joshua) the Liberator, as proclaimed in Luke 4:18-19, which repeats Isaiah 61:11. In this foundational symbol of evangelization, the Word of God comes prophetically from the oppressed margins of society to challenge spiritually its idolatrous centers of power.

This Western shift in the foundational biblical symbolic pole began hundreds of years ago, with the spiritual songs of the oppressed African-rooted peoples of the Atlantic slave system. More recently, it developed a newer Catholic expression with the Amerindian-rooted Theology of Liberation articulated by the Amerindian theologian Gustavo Gutiérrez (of Quechua-Inca ancestry). Now the Theology of Liberation is spreading ecumenically across the planet.[5]

Yet in the time of Constantine, while the Catholic bishops were re-structuring Christianity into the new Imperial Church, persecuted Christians were still suffering in imperial prisons (again, especially Coptic Christians). The older church of the martyrs and the early Imperial Church thus co-existed for some time as alternative paths for Jesus' disciples. Eventually, however, the Imperial Church won and the Age of Martyrs ended. That also ended Christianity's foundational lay era.

---

[5] Adapted from Joe Holland, "See-Judge-Act: A Praxis Method for Catholic Practical Theology," keynote address to Iannone Conference II, St. Thomas University School of Theology & Ministry, Miami Gardens, Florida, 2 May 2015. Full text available via email request from *office@paceminterris.net*.

20

At the beginning of the episcopal-imperial alliance formed in the fourth century, the Emperor Constantine gave to the Catholic bishops in many towns an imperial building for their gatherings. The Greek word for emperor is *basileus*, so those imperial buildings were called (in English translation) "basilicas," meaning buildings of the emperor. Imperial basilicas became the first large church buildings.

Prior to that gift of imperial buildings, the community of Jesus' disciples had typically gathered during three centuries for the Lord's Supper in *people's homes*. Following the donation of imperial buildings to the bishops, a tendency emerged to think of the "Church" as *holy buildings* (so today we "go to Church"), rather than as the sacred gathering of Jesus' disciples who form the holy, chosen, and priestly *Laos*.

Further, with the new alliance between the Catholic bishops and the Empire, imperial leaders extended to the bishops and to their presbyters the *special class-rank of the imperial pagan priesthood*. This special imperial class rank ("state" or "status") is the legal origin of the "clerical state." That imperial "state" legally gave to Jesus' ordained disciples *certain government-granted economic and political privileges that Jesus' non-ordained disciples did not receive* – for example, exemption from imperial taxes and from military service in the imperial army, plus a legal court only for those in the "clerical state."

Again, the Greek word *kleros*, from which the word "clergy" is derived, refers in the Greek texts of the New Testament to the "chosen" character of all disciples of Jesus who form the holy *Laos* (1 Peter 2:5-10). Yet in a non-evangelical manner, the New Testament's lay term *kleros* became misidentified with a 'higher' clerical class ruling from 'above' the *Laos* of Jesus' non-clerical disciples. As a result, a non-evangelical tendency also emerged to identify clericalized bishops and presbyters as "*the Church*," rather than the full *Laos* of all Jesus' disciples.

That Constantinian episcopal-imperial alliance then expanded geographically the Catholic evangelization of Western Civilization. It often did so, however, through military force imposed on 'uncivilized' (meaning not living in cities) European tribal peoples, and later in similar manner on 'uncivilized' non-European tribal peoples.

Along with its contributions, that late classical Greco-Roman episcopal-imperial alliance created *three anti-evangelical distortions* of the original apostolic community of Jesus' disciples.

- *Loss of Lay Identity.* First, it weakened the foundational evangelical truth that Christian church was entirely a *lay community of disciples*. It did so by promoting a wrong sense that the church was a state-sponsored institution identified with set of *temple-like buildings*, and alternately with a *hierarchical clerical class* receiving state privileges that the rest of Jesus' disciples did not receive.

- *Ruling Clerical Class.* Second, it weakened the foundational evangelical command that the ordained leaders of Jesus' disciples were to function as *servant-leaders* of the wider lay community. It did that by social construction of an imperially privileged clerical class empowered by the imperial state to *rule hierarchically over the Laos*.

- *Cross as Imperial Military Conquest.* Third, as many elite clericalized leaders supported the militaristic Roman Imperial State, a hierarchical-patriarchal and military-command style of leadership was imposed on the Catholic community. That imperial style for ecclesial leadership then undermined the foundational evangelical doctrine of the *Cross* as a symbol of persecution. That undermining not only legitimated imperial, class-based, and gender-based domination. It also inverted the meaning of the Cross *from Jesus' suffering imperial execution to supporting imperial conquest*.

As a symbol of that third distortion of Christianity, we have the legend of Constantine seeing in a vision the Cross with Greek words that have been traditionally rendered in Latin as "*In hoc signo vinces*" (Under this sign you will conquer). Thus was the prophetic meaning of the Cross of Jesus inverted. Again, no longer a sign of *persecution*, the Cross became a sign of *military conquest and domination*.

That imperial identification of evangelization with imperial violence would continue for Western Catholic Christianity up to the time of the early modern European-Catholic "*Conquista*" of the First Nations of the Americas, beginning in the late fifteenth and early sixteenth centuries. It continued during the late nineteenth and early twentieth centuries into *Modern Western Industrial Colonialism*.

Catholic examples of Modern Western Industrial Colonialism included Belgian King Leopold's personally held "Congo Free State," which caused the unjust death of perhaps ten-million people, as well as the twentieth-century 'imperial' conquest of Ethiopia by the officially 'Catholic' Italian fascist state of Benito Mussolini.

Predominantly Protestant modern examples included the vast British Empire across Africa, Asia, and the Caribbean, as well as the United States' genocidal military attacks on the First Nations of the continent – most infamously in the indigenous "Trail of Tears." It also included Modern Western Neo-Colonialism throughout Africa, the Asian/Pacific region, and the Latin American/Caribbean region.

"Cross and sword" (and later machine gun) continued in Western partnership across the 2oth Century. The most famous example occurred in the late 20th Century with the Vatican-CIA alliance, established between U.S. President Ronald Reagan and Pope John Paul II, to support the right-wing side of the "Contra Wars" in Central America. Let us hope and pray that will remain the last tragic example of the Constantinian inversion.

Coenobitical Communities
at the Margins of the Imperial Church
(300-500)

Within the classical Constantinian urban-imperial setting, the Catholic episcopal shepherds of Jesus' disciples became tempted to *lose their prophetic voice*. In response, a spiritual hunger for that prophetic voice led to the next institutional wave of Catholic spiritual energy, namely, the Desert Mothers and Desert Fathers, who eventually formed what have been called coenobitical communities.

Maurice Monette, in his pioneering book titled KINDRED SPIRITS: BONDING OF LAITY AND RELIGIOUS, has provided a helpful description of that new Catholic form of spiritual energy:

> *Lay men and women fled to into the desert to pursue the ideal life set by holy ascetics like Anthony of the Desert (251-356 CE). The desert became for them a wondrous and life-giving milieu. Their reasons for being there were varied. For the earlier hermits, the desert was often an escape from persecution and a place to seek holiness through asceticism. For many of the fiercely independent Egyptian peasants, the desert was a route to escape from insurmountable economic burdens. For yet others, the flight from the new Christian cities was a protest against the church turned too worldly and over-institutionalized, now that it was established in the Empire and no longer persecuted.*[6]

About these communities, he continues:

> *This movement began in the Egyptian desert and on the Eastern rim of the Mediterranean and gradually spread west to the Italian peninsula, Spain, Gaul, and the northern coast of Africa. It attracted men and women from all strata of society ... The coenobia*

---

[6] Maurice Monette, KINDRED SPIRITS: *Bonding of Laity and Religious* (Sheed & Ward, 1987), p. 29.

attracted thousands of ascetics, even families. Perhaps ten thousand
ascetics were networked in Egypt by Pachomius and Mary alone.[7]

Though the initial Egyptian desert movement began before the Constantinian inversion (and may even have had pre-Christian roots),
and though the motives for involvement were diverse, note especially what Maurice Monette has described above as "a protest
against a church turned too worldly and over-institutionalized, now
that it was established in the Empire and no longer persecuted." Further, in contrast to the social construction of hierarchical "clergy" for
the Imperial Church, this new form of Catholic institutional energy
remained lay. Paradoxically, however, church historians and ascetical theologians would later identify it as the first stage of "religious
life."

Return to the Wilderness

Thus, some disciples of Jesus, inspired by the Holy Spirit to live the
"Way" of discipleship more intensely, turned to the ancient human
ascetical path which rejected elite cities and the empires that grew
out of them. Those heroic disciples first heard the call to live the Cross
of Jesus in their own persons, and they abandoned life in imperial
cities. Like Israel and Jesus before them, they returned to the wilderness – that is, to Nature – in order to become closer to their Creator.
They also embraced spiritual martyrdom for their own bodies.

Again, like Israel and like Jesus, they sought to meet God in the
harshness of Nature, but also in Nature's ecological beauty. In the
natural world, they celebrated the astounding beauty of the loving
Creator's beloved creation. Like Francis of Assisi many centuries
later, they even befriended non-human animals. In that return to the
beauty of the natural world, and within it to wider animal kingdom,

---

[7] Monette, KINDRED SPIRITS, p 30.

they imagined themselves returning to the Garden of Eden's mystical Paradise.

Found especially in Egypt, Syria, and Palestine, this radical Christian movement also appeared far away in the Keltic church of Ireland, although in Ireland the radicals went not to the desert, but to forest and mountain, and to the rocky turbulence at the edge of the wild sea.

In their early stage, these Desert Mothers and Fathers have been called "*anchorites,*" which meant that they led the stable and solitary existence of hermits. As more of these radical disciples fled to the desert, however, they established the *coenobitical* form of common life. Though they often continued to be described as "hermits," perhaps their coenobitical communities were bioregional rural ecovillages.

Those coenobitical communities were the first form of special Catholic Christian mystical-prophetic intentional communities, distinct from the wider institutionalized Church of the Empire. With hindsight, we can say that their mission (at least in the Imperial period) was to be a counterpoint to Constantinian imperial urbanism, with its military-imperial inversion of the meaning of the Cross. They witnessed to the Cross by living in simple poverty and in the hardships felt by their own bodies. But they also celebrated the beauty of creation and befriended its wondrous creatures. Many reportedly embraced voluntary celibacy, yet there seemed also to have been among them large numbers of married couples with children. Again, they may have been the Christian ecovillages of the late classical period.

Thus, on one side, many episcopal authorities of the Imperial Church lost consciousness of the lay nature of the apostolic church, of its prophetic critique of the Empire, and of the identity of the Cross with persecution. On the other side, the Desert Mothers and Fathers kept alive those themes as healing gifts to the wider church and society, and they rooted their lives in the ecological beauty of Nature.

Negative Strains of Hellenist Philosophy

While the Desert Mothers and Desert Fathers drew on the Gospel of Jesus and on the Genesis narrative of Eden's Paradise, some also drew on certain negative strains in Hellenist Philosophy. As we have seen, such negative strains wrongly expressed contempt for material creation, including for the human body, for human sexuality, and especially for the body of woman (again, whom Genesis 1:27 describes as the feminine face of the "image of God").

Negative non-evangelical teachings, including Neo-Platonist and sometimes even Gnostic teachings, had long been in circulation across the Hellenistic culture that arose in the wake of the conquests of Alexander the Great (356-323 BCE). The classical center of Christian Neo-Platonist Philosophy became the North-African city of Alexandria, to which (according to the Coptic tradition) the evangelist Mark had brought Christianity, and which became a Catholic "patriarchal" city.[8]

---

[8] Plato had viewed women's mind (*psyche* or "soul") as equal to men's mind in the spiritual pursuit of wisdom (with "Philosophy," meaning from its Greek roots the "love of wisdom"). Yet Plato had also taught that the human rational "soul" (again, mind) had no gender, and that "souls" had "fallen" into, and become trapped within, human bodies, which then constituted temporary prisons for the entrapped souls. In that corporeal entrapment, however, Plato had defined *the female body as inferior to the male body*, since he ranked it lower than the male body in the descending hierarchy of reincarnation for those who failed to become enlightened philosophers. Further, the misogyny of Plato's student Aristotle became notorious, for Aristotle in his POLITICS wrote that women, as well as 'uncivilized' tribal peoples, were sub-human due to an alleged lack of rationality. Aristotle's proof that 'barbarian' tribes were not fully rational was that they viewed women and men as equals. If the 'barbarian' men were equal to 'barbarian' women, he concluded, then both must be subhuman.

On the deep Western philosophical bias against women found in the writings not only of Plato and Aristotle, but also of Descartes, Rousseau, Kant, Hume, Locke, and Hegel, see the excellent book by Nancy Tuana, WOMAN AND THE HISTORY OF PHILOSOPHY (Paragon House, 1992).

Contempt for material creation (again including for the human body, for human sexuality, and especially for women's bodies) had never been part of Jesus' teaching. Although most Christians believe that Jesus lived the spiritual creativity of the celibate vocation and even encouraged select individuals to follow that path, it is clear from the New Testament that Jesus did not combine his honoring of the charism of celibacy with contempt for material creation, nor for the human body, nor for human sexuality, nor for the body of woman.

In contrast to classical demeaning of women, Jesus held up women as the first hearers and proclaimers of the Gospel. We see this in his mother Mary's special role, in the refusal of key female disciples to flee from his crucifixion, and in his first appearance after the resurrection to Mary Magdalene, who was his most important female disciple.

Married Catholic Bishops & Presbyters

Similarly, regarding sexuality and marriage, Jesus' first public miracle was for a wedding feast, and he appears to have chosen mostly married individuals as his apostles. Continuing that apostolic precedent, for the first thousand years of Christian history the Catholic bishops and presbyters throughout the Catholic Churches, including within the Latin or Roman Church, were typically married. In early support for that later tradition, the New Testament presumes that bishops or presbyters overseeing the communities of Jesus' disciples would be married. Thus, I TIMOTHY 3:2-5 states:

> *Therefore, a bishop must be irreproachable, **married only once**, temperate, self-controlled, decent, hospitable, able to teach, not a drunkard, not aggressive, but gentle, not contentious, not a lover of money. He must manage his own household well, keeping his children under control with perfect dignity; for if a man does not know how to manage his own household, how can he take care of the church of God? (Bold font added.)*

Similarly, regarding presbyters, TITUS 1:5-7 states:

> *Appoint presbyters in every town, as I directed you, on condition that a man be blameless, **married only once**, with believing children who are not accused of licentiousness or rebellious. For a bishop as God's steward must be blameless, not arrogant, not irritable, not a drunkard, not aggressive, not greedy for sordid gain. (Bold font added.)*[9]

Over against perhaps hundreds of later Western Catholic theological volumes defending the Western Catholic Church's second-millennium law of mandatory "clerical celibacy" for its bishops and presbyters, the clear teaching of the New Testament must certainly rank higher. In addition, of the twenty-four "*sui-juris*" Catholic churches that make up the global Catholic family in communion with the Catholic Bishop of Rome, with many having apostolic origin, practically all those churches have never required "clerical celibacy" for their presbyters.

Jesus' Cosmic Spirituality

Jesus' spirituality was not anti-worldly but rather *Earth-rooted*, celebrating the birds of the air and the lilies of the field. Further, Jesus proclaimed an *eschatological renewal of all creation* that would include both the "Heavens" and the "Earth." Contrary to the Pythagorean, Platonic, and Neo-Platonist goals of only "saving souls," Jesus did not preach "saving souls." Rather, he proclaimed a "Paradise" that would include resurrected bodies and eschatological renewal of both the "Heavens and Earth," that is, of the entire Cosmos.[10]

---

[9] The above biblical quotations are from the NEW AMERICAN BIBLE. Note that, in the beginning of Christianity, bishops and presbyters were not clearly distinguished.

[10] See Rebecca Ann Parker & Rita Nakashima Brock, SAVING PARADISE: *How Christianity Traded Love of this World for Empire and Crucifixion* (Beacon Press, 2009).

After the foundational first centuries, however, non-evangelical and anti-material Hellenistic teachings began to infect Catholic spirituality. As a result, non-evangelical teachings – again, disparaging material creation, disparaging the human body, disparaging human sexuality, and especially disparaging the body of woman – spread across significant aspects of *classical Catholic Ascetical Theology*. That infection has continued in some sectors even up to today.

Disintegration of the Western Empire

The historical mission of the communities of Desert Mothers and Fathers made sense as a prophetic counter-point only so long as the clericalized episcopal and presbyteral authorities in the Roman imperial cities remained as religious functionaries of the Empire. Yet with the growing migrations of 'barbarian' German tribes into the Western Empire, with their military attacks on many Western imperial cities, and with the slow but relentless internal breakdown of the Western imperial organization, the Roman Empire in the West gradually fell into turmoil and decline.

Many historians have judged that, by the end of the fifth century, the Western Empire had ceased to exist, though some imperial structures continued beyond that point, and many migrating tribes integrated Roman traditions into their cultures.[11] Even so, with imperial decline, coenobitical communities in the West lost a key *raison d'être*.

---

[11] The Eastern Roman Empire, known also as the Byzantine Empire and centered in the then Greek city of Constantinople, survived until its conquest by the Ottoman Turks in 1453.

Monastic Communities
Rebuilding Civilization within Feudalism
(500-1200)

As Feudalism replaced Empire in the West, a new Western wave of "religious life" called "*monasticism*" displaced the historical role of coenobitical communities as the dominant historical form of Catholic mystical-prophetic intentional communities.

To repeat, as migrating 'barbarian' German tribes triumphed across Western Europe, they plundered imperial cities, which people then often abandoned. For survival, many people returned to rural areas and joined fortified enclaves, which became the new "feudal" form of Western European society. Decentralized and ruled over by patriarchal-aristocratic warlords, peasants in those fortified rural communities were bound in oaths of fealty to their warlords.

Within that historical context, the new strategic question for prophetic leaders within the Western Catholic community became how to evangelize the migrating 'barbarian' German tribes, and with them how to rebuild Western Christian Civilization. The strategic response of Catholic spiritual energy became the post-imperial stage of *Western monasticism*. That development represented a historically new spiritual-institutional form for Catholic Christianity, even though other forms of monasticism had existed earlier within Buddhism in the East and in Mediterranean Pythagorean communities.

Irish-Keltic Monasticism

Following the fall of the Western Empire, the migrating German tribes settled in Western rural areas along with the existing Western tribal peoples, including Keltic tribes that had migrated earlier from Asia Minor. In response to that new social situation, the Keltic church in Ireland sent highly educated male monks from the Irish tribes – and often from royal or aristocratic families – as nomadic missionaries to convert, and to educate, the migrating German tribes. Those Irish-Keltic monks then worked with royal and aristocratic leaders of the German tribes to create the new medieval form of Western Christian Civilization.[12]

Again, the Keltic missionaries were often sons of royal or aristocratic Irish families. Further, formed in the great Irish monastic schools of higher education, they brought with them advanced training in Philosophy, Theology, and the Liberal Arts, including fluency in both

---

[12] Most histories of Western monasticism unfortunately give only a brief and poorly informed account of the great work of the Irish-Keltic evangelization and education of the German tribes in Western Europe. For a popular account of the intellectual-spiritual role of Irish-Keltic monasticism in evangelizing Western Europe and regenerating Western Civilization, see Thomas Cahill, HOW THE IRISH SAVED CIVILIZATION: *The Story of Ireland's Heroic Role from the Fall of Rome to the Rise of Medieval Europe* (Anchor, 1996). For an older and more extensively researched analysis of that achievement, see Benedict Fitzpatrick's two detailed studies, IRELAND AND THE MAKING OF BRITAIN (Funk & Wagnalls, 1922) and IRELAND AND THE FOUNDATIONS OF EUROPE (Funk & Wagnalls, 1927). Both of Fitzpatrick's books (originally planned to be one book) are based especially on Fitzpatrick's continental research of manuscripts in the Irish language. (His second book was the source for Peter Maurin's three-part "Green Revolution.")

Scholarly neglect of the impact of Irish-Keltic monasticism in standard histories of Western monasticism may be partly due to lack of research into manuscripts in the Irish language. It may also be the result of marginalization of the Irish-Keltic Church by the Imperial Roman Church (similar to what happened to the "Donatist" African Coptic Church), and of subsequent destruction of Irish manuscripts within Ireland by Viking plundering and still later by British Protestant imperialism. Saint Augustine of Hippo (354-430) also contributed to the initial marginalization of the Irish-Keltic Christian tradition across continental Europe by his promotion of the Imperial Church. That happened especially through his polemic against the Irish-Keltic lay theologian Pelagius, who was his brilliant competitor for intellectual-spiritual influence in Roman aristocratic circles. (Some contemporary scholars have argued that Pelagius was not a "Pelagian.") Later, the Roman-directed Synod of Whitby (664) weakened Keltic monasticism in England, in favor of the organizational model of the Latin Benedictine monasticism favored by the Imperial Church. Still later, and more ruthlessly, the seventeenth-century social and intellectual devastation of Ireland by the English Puritan military conqueror Oliver Cromwell included a campaign to destroy all Irish monastic libraries, and to burn all manuscripts written in the Irish language. It became a capital offense even to possess a manuscript written in Irish.

Greek and Latin, and knowledge of classical works like the writings of Cicero. Other Keltic monks from across the British Isles (typically trained in the Irish monastic schools of higher education) also participated in the great Keltic mission to continental Europe.

While Latin Church intellectuals of that time were ignorant of Greek (Saint Augustine of Hippo, for example, could never learn it), the Irish-Keltic scholars carried a long tradition of fluency in Greek, and they were well schooled in the classical Greek intellectual legacy. It appears that the early Irish-Keltic Church may have been closer to the Byzantine Greek Church, and perhaps also to the African Coptic Church with its vast coenobitical movement, than to the Roman Latin Church.

That may be understandable, since the Keltic tribes had migrated out of Asia Minor, and there had been an ancient Keltic presence close to Greece. For example, in the region that is today's Turkey, the ancient province of Galatia (to whose Church Saint Paul wrote an epistle) had been Keltic. Also, a Keltic army once almost conquered Athens.

Sharing their sophisticated education with the German tribes advancing across Western Europe, the Irish-Keltic missionaries founded monasteries, promoted agriculture, built libraries and schools, and established towns. For example, the Austrian city of Vienna honors its development by Irish-Keltic monks. Further, Irish-Keltic scholars became famous at the Merovingian and Carolingian courts.

While earlier Latin missionaries had failed in their attempt to convert the German tribes, the Irish-Keltic missionaries became immediately successful – again, probably because they themselves came from tribal communities, and often carried aristocratic or even royal rank. The Irish-Keltic monks, together with leaders of the newly evangelized German tribes, then laid the intellectual and spiritual foundations for medieval Europe.

Thus, though seldom fully explored in standard Western Christian histories, the first expanding form of Western Christian monasticism within Europe, and the early source for re-founding Western Christian Civilization after the decline of the Western Roman Empire, was the Irish-Keltic monastic evangelization and education of the German tribes. Irish-Keltic missionary foundations in Europe were not places where monks left society, but rather places where monks and local tribal leaders worked together to rebuild civilization. Their monasteries became creative centers of spiritual, social, and intellectual regeneration, and places where Western Christian Civilization began to grow anew.

Meanwhile, in Ireland from which the monks came, Keltic monasticism had long provided stable communities for women and men. In contrast to the Roman Latin model, Irish-Keltic Catholic Christians, like the original apostolic church, celebrated salvation as embracing Nature, and welcomed the leadership of strong women. Female abbesses often led closely connected male and female Keltic monasteries.

Further, in Ireland the Keltic Church had identified its monasteries not with stone buildings but rather with the beauty of Nature, as in the lush green valley of the ancient Irish-Keltic monastery of Glendalough (Valley of Two Lakes), founded within the gentle Wicklow Mountains during the sixth century by Saint Kevin. Reportedly, during the so-called European "Dark Ages," thousands of young people came every summer from the continent to study with the Irish-Keltic monks in the lush green monastic valley of Glendalough.

In addition, Thomas Cahill has claimed that the Irish-Keltic Catholic Church saw the prophetic critique of social injustice as central to the Gospel of Jesus and to authentic evangelization (in contrast to the Imperial Church, which moved away from the prophetic biblical tradition). In that regard, Saint Patrick, active in Ireland in the fifth century (after Christianity had been established in the South of that land) was captured as a youth by Irish pirates, and then became enslaved in Ireland. In that experience, he had learned first-hand of the terrible nature of slavery, and especially for women.

Benedictine Latin Monasticism

In a manner softer than the strongly ascetical style of Keltic monasticism, Saint Benedict of Norcia (480-543), son of a feudal lord in the Italian peninsula, developed the Latin form of monasticism that would later become the dominant Western European Catholic model. At the same time, his twin sister Saint Scholastica (480-453) founded a female branch of the order. But Benedict and Scholastica did not have a program for missionary outreach the invading German tribes.

Eventually, however, Benedictine monasticism displaced Irish-Keltic Monasticism in Europe and, in some cases, became complicit in the restoration of imperial consciousness within the Roman Church. From that point on, the Nature-oriented Irish-Keltic stream of Christian spirituality – continuing mainly at the Western margins of European civilization – would not broadly re-emerge with spiritual power until the late 20th Century. It was retrieved then in spiritual response to the profound global ecological crisis that grew in part out of the spiritual errors planted within the dualist-hierarchical ground of what became clericalized monastic spirituality.

In the interim, however, so powerful became the influence of some forms of Benedictine monasticism on the emerging European society that the great German sociologist Max Weber claimed that Modern Capitalism was an outgrowth of Benedictine monasticism's early spiritual-technological rationalization. We might say that, in his classic book, THE PROTESTANT ETHIC AND THE SPIRIT OF CAPITALISM (1905), while implicitly arguing that John Calvin (1509-1564), founder of the Calvinist strain of Protestantism, was the 'father' of modern Capitalism, Weber implicitly argued that Benedict was the 'grandfather.'

Benedictine monasteries were originally spiritual centers of egalitarian community, presided over by loving feudal patriarchs called "abbots" (from the Hebrew word *abba*, meaning "father"). As their mission succeeded, however, some Benedictine monasteries, particularly the European monastic network of Cluny, became a powerful political-economic force of aristocratic hierarchy within Europe.

During the 'high' Middle Ages, the Benedictine community of monastic lay disciples, originally sharing together in the mutual tasks of *ora et labora* (prayer and labor), became dualistically and hierarchically divided. On one side were aristocratic "*choir monks*" of the "religious state" who were assigned to *ora*. On the other side were lower-class "*lay monks*" who were assigned to *labora*. Further, the wealthy monasteries of Cluny also hired lower-class lay workers to do the "*labora*," while the choir monks – supposedly devoted exclusively to prayer – developed luxurious lifestyles. That more 'developed' model of Western monasticism forgot the evangelical character of the apostolic church's original Christian *Laos*.

Centuries later, in Benedictine monastic foundations within the English Midlands, lower-class lay employees also replaced lower-class lay monks as workers. Those monastic lands in the Midlands, devoted to the profitable task of raising sheep to obtain wool for textiles, later became "secularized" by King Henry VIII. Still later, that same region became the English seedbed for the modern Industrial Revolution, in which textiles played a central role.

Forgetting Sacred Immanence

Though Benedictine monasticism included separate male and female monasteries, it did not include the sacrament of Christian Marriage. Further, the dominant male side eventually centered itself in the masculine spiritual symbol of *sacred transcendence*, seeking to rise 'above' Nature – again, with lower-class lay brothers and lower-class lay employees assigned to deal with the 'lower' tasks of Nature. As a result, certain strains of Western male monasticism tended to forget the Divine revelation in Nature of the primal feminine spiritual symbol of *sacred immanence.*

Further, since Benedictine monasticism also became in the Classical Era the center of Western or Roman Catholic Theology, many teachers of the Western Roman Church theologically emphasized *sacred transcendence* as the masculine symbol of the Divine Mystery. Some later identified that male face of the Divine with men in the "clerical" and "religious" "states of life." By this time, upper-level monks were typically being ordained priests and became part of the hierarchical "clergy."

Major strains of male Benedictine monasticism, oriented to masculinized "religious" and "clerical" transcendence, gained great patriarchal political-economic power in the high Middle Ages. Again, the rich and powerful monasteries of Cluny – for a time the greatest landowner in Europe – began to reshape the papacy in the name of 'reform.'

Misogynist Contempt for Women

In their 'reforming' zeal for masculine transcendence, some Western monastic leaders from Cluny attempted to impose a Platonic antisexual model of hierarchical dualism on diocesan bishops and diocesan presbyters. In a cruel attack on the Catholic families of traditionally married Western Catholic bishops and presbyters, and on their Catholic wives and children, one pope of that time, inspired by the monasticism of Cluny, declared "clerical marriages *"heretical."* That theologically claim became a source of great tension with the Eastern Churches, which rejected such an anti-evangelical absurdity.

The forced imposition of the monastic celibate model on diocesan bishops and presbyters became the central task of the so-called "Gregorian Reform," identified especially by the Pope Gregory VII (Bishop of Rome from 1073 to 1085). Known earlier as Hildebrand,

Gregory had been formed by the monasticism of Cluny. As pope, Gregory tried to force by coercive police-power all Western bishops and presbyters, who had continued the thousand-year old tradition of Christian marriage, *to abandon their Christian wives and their Christian children.*[13]

A central part of this brutal anti-evangelical campaign was an underlying *misogynist contempt for women.* The contemporary historian Anne Llewellyn Barstow reported that the monastic-inspired papal campaign not only forcibly removed the wives of bishops and presbyters from their homes, but also often drove displaced wives into homelessness, prostitution, and even suicide. Barstow has described that violent papal attack on the traditional marriage and families of Catholic bishops and presbyters as the "monasticizing of the clergy."[14]

Further, Anne Llewellyn Barstow and the earlier historian Henry Lea, both distinguished scholars, stated that written records of resistance by traditionally married bishops and traditionally married presbyters suggested that there was a medieval homosexual clerical culture behind the 'reforming' attack on "clerical marriage."

The late and distinguished Yale historian John Boswell, in his celebrated work, CHRISTIANITY, SOCIAL TOLERANCE, AND HOMOSEXUALITY, famously pointed to a broad late classical and medieval "clerical" tolerance of homosexuality.[15] Yet it was during this same period of "tolerance" that the monastic-driven papal attack on the Christian marriages and families of Western bishops and presbyters occurred.

---

[13] On this period, see the classic study by Henry C. Lea, HISTORY OF SACERDOTAL CELIBACY IN THE CHRISTIAN CHURCH (Kessinger Publishing, 2003), with the original published in 1867. Lea once served as president of the American Historical Society.

[14] Anne Llewellyn Barstow, MARRIED PRIESTS AND THE REFORMING PAPACY: *The 11th Century Debates* (Edwin Mellen, 1982). The phrase "monasticizing of the clergy" appears throughout the book.

[15] John Boswell, CHRISTIANITY, SOCIAL TOLERANCE, AND HOMOSEXUALITY: *Gay People in Western Europe from the Beginning of the Christian Era to the Fourteenth Century* (University of Chicago Press, 2005).

Why tolerance on one side, but not on the other? In response to that question, Barstow has summarized Boswell's honest narrative:

The Gregorian church ... in the century 1050-1150 created no legislation against gay clergy. Indeed, it has been argued that this was a period in which homosexuality flourished among clerics, especially in monasteries, and that since monks gained the ascendency in the church at this time, the legislative centers of the church had little choice but to go light on the question of men who loved men.

John Boswell claims that St. Anselm and several of his pupils, Pope Alexander II and Archbishop Lanfranc, Archbishop Ralph of Tours and his beloved "Flora," Bishop John of Orléans, Bishop William Longchamp of Ely, and most notably Ailred of Rievaulx and his Simon, all represent influential churchmen whose actions and/or writings help make this century notable for clerical homosexuality.

Boswell goes so far as to claim that "there was more than a coincidental relation between gay sexuality and some of the [celibacy] reforms ... A satire against a reforming bishop specifically accuses him of hostility to clerical marriage because of his own homosexual disposition." There is some evidence of a power struggle between gay and married clergy over whose predilections would be stigmatized. Indeed, we will see that several [medieval] married clerical authors will express themselves vehemently on just that point.[16]

Both Barstow and Lea's studies also reveal a hate-filled misogynist language from leaders of that 'reform.' Perhaps the worst known examples came from Pietro Damiani (c. 1007-1072), a Benedictine monk, later cardinal, still later a declared saint, and at the time lead papal agent of the Gregorian attack on the Catholic marriages and Catholic families of Western bishops and presbyters. Damiani's vicious words

---

[16] Barstow, MARRIED PRIESTS, pp. 113-114; Boswell, CHRISTIANITY, pp. 210-227.

betray a horrendous contempt for women, and especially for the female body. As an example, Barstow has cited one of Damiani's many "fulminations" against the Catholic women who shared in the apostolic tradition of married bishops and presbyters:

> *I speak to you, o charmers of the clergy, appetizing flesh of the devil, that casting away from paradise, you, poison of the minds, death of souls, companions of the very stuff of sin, the cause of our ruin. You, I say, I exhort you women of the ancient enemy, you bitches, sows, screech-owls, night owls, she-wolves, blood-suckers ... Come now, hear me, harlots, prostitutes, with your lascivious kisses, you wallowing places for fat pigs, couches for unclean spirits, demigoddesses, sirens, witches.*
>
> *You vipers full of madness, parading the ardor of your ungovernable lust, through your lovers you mutilate Christ, who is the head of the clergy ... you snatch away the unhappy men from their ministry of the sacred altar ... that you may strangle them in the slimy glue of your passion ... The ancient foe pants to invade the summit of the church's chastity through you ...* **They should kill you.**[17] *(Bold font added.)*

In other "tirades" against the wives of presbyters and bishops, Damiani repeated his hatred for women:

> *The hands that touch the body and blood of Christ must not have touched the genitals of a whore ... I have attempted to place the restraints of continence upon the genitals of the priesthood, upon those who have the high honor of touching the body and blood of Christ.*[18]

---

[17] Cited by Barstow, MARRIED PRIESTS, pp. 60-61.

[18] Cited by Barstow, MARRIED PRIESTS, pp. 59-60.

Yet Barstow also told a story about how Damiani's own mother, after his birth, had refused to nurse him, and only the intervention of a priest's wife had saved the baby.

> *As the infant Peter lay withering away, an angel of mercy came from an unexpected and ... ironic source: a neighboring priest's wife took pity on the starving infant and talked his mother into offering him her breast, thereby saving the life of the future scourge of priestly families.*[19]

In the misogynist language of that monastic-led papal 'reform,' we see clearly the infection of Western Catholic spirituality by the negative teachings still flowing from certain anti-material philosophical schools within Hellenism. Again, these negative teachings disparaged material creation, disparaged the human body, disparaged human sexuality, and especially disparaged the body of woman.

Barstow further pointed out that ecclesiastical decrees, at the papal and at regional levels, ordered that the wives and children of married clerics should be *sold into slavery*.[20] Lea also documented that Pope Leo IX (1049-1054) had ordered the enslavements of presbyters' wives when the couple refused to be separated. Leo, also a promoter of the power of Cluny, brought Hildebrand with him to Rome and, according to Lea, dramatically "magnified" the distinction between "clergy and laity."[21]

Similarly, Lea noted, Pope Urban II (1088-1099) – a follower of the Gregorian 'reform,' founder of the modern papal Curia, and launcher of the first medieval military "crusade" – ordered 'recalcitrant' clerical wives into slavery. He further noted that Urban even "offered their

---

[19] Barstow, MARRIED PRIESTS, pp. 58-59.

[20] Barstow, MARRIED PRIESTS, p. 43.

[21] Lea, HISTORY OF SACERDOTAL CELIBACY, p. 154.

servitude as a bribe to the nobles who should aid in thus purifying the Church."[22]

Also, the historian Earl Evelyn Sperry, dating the "beginning of a crusade against the married clergy" to 1049 (first year of Leo IX's papacy) and describing Pietro Damiani as "principal instigator," pointed out that:

> *A council at Rome decreed that the wives of the clergy should be attached as slaves to the Lateran Palace, and bishops of the church were urged to inflict the same punishments upon the wives of priests.*

In addition, Sperry reported that later the "Hungarian Council of Ofen (1279) enacted that the children of ecclesiastics should be the slaves of the church."[23]

Papal Lust for Theocratic Imperial Power

Ultimately, according to Sperry, what stood behind the cruel 'reform' was the monastic-inspired papal lust for theocratic imperial power. Thus, Sperry wrote:

> *With the election of Hildebrand to the Papal chair ... a celibate clergy was indispensable to a realization of his views concerning the position of the Pope in the affairs of the world. His theories are clearly set forth in the DICTATUS PAPAE ... This enunciation of Papal rights ... is tantamount to a declaration that the Pope is the autocrat of the church.*

---

[22] Lea, HISTORY OF SACERDOTAL CELIBACY, p. 198.

[23] For both preceding quotes, see Earl Evelyn Sperry, AN OUTLINE OF THE HISTORY OF CLERICAL CELIBACY IN WESTERN EUROPE TO THE COUNCIL OF TRENT (Doctoral Dissertation for Columbia University, 1905), pp. 41-43. The author had been a University Fellow at Columbia University and later became a professor of history at Syracuse University.

As to the powers of the Pope in secular affairs, Gregory declared that he might depose emperors, that he might annul the decrees of all earthly authorities, but that no one could annul Papal decrees, and that he was to be judged by no one. [According to] the DICTATUS PAPAE *... all earthly rulers and powers are amenable and subordinate to the pope ...*

Sperry continued:

As spiritual chief of the world, it was necessary that the Pope should have for his agents a body of men without local attachments and without personal interests to which they might sacrifice the welfare of the church. It was necessary that their powers should be devoted exclusively to defense and aggrandizement of this great ecclesial institution.

To create a body of men with such singleness of purpose, it was also necessary, besides cutting of all personal interest, to distinguish them sharply from the people they were to rule. The indelible spiritual attributes conferred at ordination accomplished this to some degree, but celibacy was a much more obvious and striking distinction. ... [Celibacy would] deprive the clergy of the cares, ambitions, and interests which the rearing of a family involves, and it would isolate them from their fellow men.[24]

Lea concurred with this analysis:

Hildebrand ... had conceived a scheme of hierarchical autocracy ... To the realization of this ideal he devoted his life with a fiery zeal and unshaken purpose that shrank from no obstacle, and to it he was ready to sacrifice not only the [people] who stood in his path, but also the immutable principles of truth and justice ... Such a man could comprehend the full importance of the rule of celibacy, not alone as essential to the ascetic purity of the Church, but as

---

[24] Sperry, OUTLINE, pp. 26-27.

necessary to the theocratic structure which he proposed to elevate on the ruins of kingdoms and empires.[25]

Key figures related to Cluny became papal leaders in the misogynist campaign against clerical families. They did so in support of the Gregorian lust for theocratic power. Meanwhile, baptized Catholic wives of bishops and priests, their baptized and ordained Catholic husbands, and their baptized Catholic children, all became victims of misogynist lust for clerical power.

How sad the apparent medieval battle between "gay" and "straight" "clergy." In that case for the "clerical" world at least, the "gay" side won, and the non-evangelical legacy of canonically mandatory "clerical" celibacy became institutionalized in the West.[26] In the wider society over longer history, however, the "straight" prejudice against "gay" people would inflict viciousness and hatred on "gay" people. Yet all persons on both sides are our loving Creator's beloved children, and all persons on both sides bear the image of the Creator's beauty and goodness.

There were other important issues in the Gregorian reform, especially the debate over lay-investiture and the papal-imperial struggle. Nonetheless, there is no question about the misogyny. And there is no question that the papacy rejected the ancient and broad apostolic tradition of married bishops and presbyters, which is affirmed by the

---

[25] Lea, HISTORY, pp. 181-182.

[26] The "clerical state" and mandatory celibacy on one side, and the Sacrament of Ordination on the other side, are distinct matters. The Western Catholic canonical requirement of celibacy is linked not to ordination but to the clerical state. That distinction and that linkage are clear from the fact that an ordained clerical celibate presbyter in the Roman Church may be released from celibacy by "reduction" to the "lay state" (*reducionem ad statum laicalem,* in Latin rescripts for "laicization"). Yet even after that "reduction," the individual remains a validly and permanently ordained presbyter, though he is forbidden to function as such. In addition, as noted, neither the "clerical state" nor mandatory celibacy for ordained presbyters are of apostolic origin.

New Testament and which continues, at least for presbyters, in practically all of the Eastern Catholic Churches.

Misogynist Influence on
Modern Science & Technology

The misogynist spiritual infection of some sectors of medieval monasticism contributed indirectly yet still powerfully to the modern hyper-masculine symbolic-mythic deformation lodged within the cultural foundations of Modern Science and Modern Philosophy. For Modern Science, originally called "Natural Philosophy" and a key carrier of Modernity's hyper-masculine deformation, arose from medieval male monasteries, even though it broke out into a lay "secular" form beyond that originally narrow ecclesial framework.

In his impressive study, A WORLD WITHOUT WOMEN: *The Clerical Origin of Western Science*, the late M.I.T. historian of technology David Noble documented the intellectual roots of the West's "New Science" in medieval Latin monasticism.[27] In that book, Noble showed how important sectors of the medieval Latin monastic movement became the incubator of Modern Science's hyper-masculine culture.

Noble had been investigating the question of why there has been a hyper-masculine deformation in the foundational style of modern Western Science, which then led Western Civilization into its contemporary unsustainable ecological degeneration. Of course, Noble found earlier roots of that deformation in the classical Greco-Roman philosophical tradition. But, he argued, medieval monasticism became the immediate source for Modern Science.

Further, there also emerged an early modern Western scientific-technological vision which intensified the medieval monastic symbolic deformation with its own misogynist strains. As the distinguished

---

[27] David Noble, A WORLD WITHOUT WOMEN: THE CLERICAL ORIGIN OF WESTERN SCIENCE (Oxford University Press, 1993).

historian of Science Carolyn Merchant has shown, Francis Bacon adopted a misogynist metaphor, metaphorically linked to techniques of torture, to describe the modern 'masculine' scientific project of forcing 'feminine' Nature to reveal her "secrets." In addition, Descartes infamously justified the 'scientific' torture of non-human animals, on grounds that they were simply machines without feeling.

Carolyn Merchant has documented the intellectual construction of that disturbing misogynist mythic-symbolic strain for Modern Science in her indicting study, THE DEATH OF NATURE: *Women, Ecology, and the Scientific Revolution*.[28]

Thus, it should not be surprising that now, within the terminal "climax" of hyper-masculine Western Modernity, we discover that the modern Western bourgeois scientific-technological path of Scientific Materialism has become ecologically *unsustainable* throughout its natural, human, and spiritual dimensions. Again, that hyper-masculine scientific-technological drive has been achieving dramatic increases in *human technological production*, but it has been destroying *Nature's biological reproduction*.

Postmodern Renewal of
Monasticism's Regenerative Charism

Of course, that monastic-inspired misogyny and theocratic-imperial lust for power of the 'Gregorian Reform' do not belong to the core of the ancient and still important monastic movement. The brutal

---

[28] In addition to her already noted book DEATH OF NATURE, see again her subsequent and already noted ISIS article, in which she persuasively defends against denying critics her claim that Bacon was using a metaphor linked to torture as the mythic-symbolic ground for the "New Science." By the way, the brilliant Irish scientist, theologian, and Anglican priest Alister McGrath, in his otherwise excellent book THE REENCHANTMENT OF NATURE: *The Denial of Religion* (Doubleday/Galilee, 2002), dismisses Carolyn Merchant's claim. But he does not seem to be familiar with the subsequent and persuasive defense of that claim in her ISIS article.

Gregorian campaign against Catholic episcopal and presbyteral families stands as a pathological deformation of the monastic charism.

Fortunately, following the medieval triumph of Cluny, zeal for retrieving the true monastic charism arose especially in the medieval Cistercian and Carthusian movements. But like Cluny and in contrast to the earlier desert movement, they remained sexually segregated communities, predominately of men, and did not include families.

Jumping far ahead to today, note that the 20th Century Catholic prophet, Peter Maurin, proposed a fresh lay and agroecological monastic movement. In Peter's vision, that lay form of the monastic movement would retrieve the civilization-building mission of the early medieval Irish-Keltic missionary scholars. It would also welcome women and men, both single and married, as well as families with children.

In my earlier book POSTMODERN ECOLOGICAL SPIRITUALITY, I proposed that a postmodern lay and agroecological monasticism, similar to Peter Maurin envisioned, needs to become a central component of the global Catholic, as well as more broadly Christian and universally human, strategic response to the late modern devastation of life's integral ecology across its interwoven planetary, human, and spiritual fabric. Again, that natural, human, and spiritual devastation is now being inflicted on the evolving creative communion of life by technological projects of late modern economistic Neoliberalism and militarist Neoconservatism, both of which embody the voluntarist philosophy of Nietzschean Nihilism.

I also proposed that his postmodern lay and agroecological Catholic monasticism needs to recover its eco-spiritual roots in "Mother Earth." In addition, it needs to support marginalized people by developing with them sustainable agroecological communities. In addition, it needs to create a regenerative agroecological model of education, grounded in the ecological wisdom of Nature, as well as in ancient peasant eco-spiritual traditions, and in the contemporary eco-logical spirituality being developed by postmodern mystics. Finally, it would hold up both the Sacrament of Marriage and the vocation of celibacy in a co-creative eco-spiritual partnership.

Again, the original form of this vision first appeared in the Catholic Worker movement's three-part "Green Revolution," as articulated by Peter Maurin in the first half of the 20th Century. As we have seen, Peter looked back to the early medieval program of Catholic evange-lization and philosophical-theological renewal developed by mis-sionary Irish-Keltic missionary scholars, in partnership with leaders of the migrating German tribes.

Though Peter had been a member of a "religious order" (the De La Salle Christian Brothers), he preferred to describe those Irish-Keltic missionaries in lay terms as "scholars," rather than as "monks." He saw those "scholars" as integrating prayer, study, and agriculture (*"cult, culture, and cultivation"*), and not simply for monks, but more broadly for rural village communities ("communes"). Further, disil-lusioned by contemporary universities and even by many Catholic-university professors, Peter called for his lay monasticism of a "Green Revolution" to create *"agronomic universities"* (that is, integrated with rural agriculture).

Today, we might better describe Peter Maurin's lay ecological mo-nasticism as grounded in rural "ecovillages" and "agroecological uni-versities," and as still serving the poor and abandoned human sisters and brothers in urban centers through what Peter called "houses of hospitality" – though these could be further developed in larger pro-jects of community development.[29]

---

[29] For one impressive example of community development with poor and marginal-ized people, see Joe & Stephanie Mancini, TRANSITION TO COMMON WORK: *Building Community at The Working Center* (Wilfred Laurier Press, 2015). The book reports on their work in Kitchener, Ontario in Canada.

Medieval Seeds of
the Modern Bourgeois Era

Now, let us return to the medieval period. With medieval monastic celibate "clerical" power guiding the 'reforming' 11th Century papacy, the papacy expanded its theocratic power over Western Europe and beyond. Within that development, medieval popes – again, in alliance with powerful monasteries of Cluny – supported great military campaigns to invade the Middle East, and they did so in the name of the Gospel. Those "Crusades" – paradoxically named after the "Cross" (*Crux* in Latin) of the non-violent Jesus – opened major commercial trading routes between West and East, which then led to the *rise of wealthy bourgeois classes* within medieval commercial cities.

Out of those medieval bourgeois classes, there later arose the modern bourgeois *"secular"* vision of society. It was earlier Neo-Platonist strains in Christian monasticism, however, that had first defined the material world as "secular." That secular vision eventually led to the bourgeois destruction of the aristocratic civilization of Christendom. In its place, elites within the rising Western lay bourgeoisie then constructed – first in liberal-capitalist form, and later in the alternative scientific-socialist form – Modern Industrial Civilization based on *Scientific Materialism,* and not reverencing matter but plundering it.

Correlatively, alongside the medieval development of bourgeois lay-secular classes, there also emerged a new post-monastic form of Catholic mystical-prophetic communities. Those communities prophetically challenged anti-evangelical and anti-human elements within the early bourgeois urban-capitalist culture of the expanding medieval mercantile city-states, and they contributed to its intellectual development through their work in emerging Western Catholic universities.

Mendicant Communities
Challenging Medieval Bourgeois Culture
(1200-1500)

The high-medieval trading cities, grown rich from the "silk roads" re-opened by Crusades, became the *young bourgeois seeds* of the modern mercantile-capitalist form of Western Civilization. Still small and living like little islands within a sea of Feudalism, those cities became the early seedbeds of both modern bourgeois political democracy and modern bourgeois materialist culture.

Meanwhile, Benedictine monks, bound to rural monasteries by once relevant vow of stability, proved unable to provide the mobile, dynamic, and flexible forms of evangelization needed for the growing medieval bourgeois urban centers, with their prosperous bourgeois families. In particular, rural monks were unable to evangelize the many young males flocking to the new urban bourgeois educational institutions eventually known as "*universities*." (Of course, in that still patriarchal culture, women were not permitted to attend such schools.)

The Mendicant Model

In response to the new historical-societal situation, there emerged the "*mendicant*" (from the Latin *mendicare*, which means "to beg") model of Catholic mystical-prophetic intentional communities. Rejecting the corporate wealth and magnificent buildings of the great monastic foundations, the new model initially embraced both individual and corporate poverty. The initial commitment to institutional poverty would erode, however, in the model's later development. Even so, the mendicant movement represented a new spiritual response to the new societal challenge from the seminally modern high-medieval bourgeois society.

The high-medieval development of the "mendicant" form of Catholic mystical-prophetic intentional communities planted seeds for an evangelical challenge to foundational evils already present in that early bourgeois culture – evils later to emerge more powerfully in Modern Western Industrial-Colonial Civilization. Those bourgeois evils included psychological and technological alienation from *Nature*, exploitation and marginalization of the *poor*, and erosion of the Socratic tradition of seeking *truth* beyond the empirical level.

Francis & Dominic

In response to the new bourgeois challenge, Giovanni de Pietro di Bernadone (c. 1181-1226) – son of a wealthy medieval bourgeois capitalist merchant and today known in English as Saint Francis of Assisi – became the founder of one new leading forms of Catholic mystical-prophetic intentional communities.

That version was eventually identified in Latin as the *Ordo Fratrum Minorum*. It is now translated into English as the "Order of Friars Minor," though the social meaning of the Latin name remains disputed. It is popularly known as the "Franciscans." Further, though beginning as a lay movement, Francis' initiative later developed into what are today known as the "first, second, and third orders," with the first a "clerical" order, the second an order of "religious" sisters, and the third an order of laity.

In troubadour style, Saint Francis built on the Nature-spirituality of the earlier Christian hermit-movement that grew into coenobitical life and survived into the medieval period. Like his hermit predecessors, he celebrated the beauteous creatures of Nature, befriended them, even preached to them, and continued the ancient Christian cosmic spirituality that saw all of creation as praising the Creator.

In addition, Francis developed a unique *Christian mysticism of the natural world,* in which, like many indigenous peoples, he identified all creatures as "brothers" and "sisters." He also lovingly embraced poor and rejected human creatures.[30]

Similarly, Domingo Félix de Guzmán Garcés (1170-1221), known today in English as Saint Dominic, became the founder of another model form, known in Latin as the *Ordo Predicatorum* (Order of Preachers) and popularly called the "Dominicans." These mendicants moved among the people, preached in vernacular languages, and soon promoted for Catholic Christianity Aristotelian scholarship, learned from African-Muslim, Jewish, and Catholic scholars in the south of Spain.[31]

Especially through Saint Thomas Aquinas (1225-1274), the Dominicans shifted the philosophical foundation of the Western Catholic theologian tradition from Platonism to Aristotelianism. In addition, they introduced the modern democratic principle into their organizational life – electing a term-limited "*prior*" (first, among equals), rather than being ruled in the classical Benedictine monastic and aristocratic-patriarchal manner by a life-time "abbot" (again, from the Hebrew *abba*, meaning "father").

New Mendicant Mission

Following the new mendicant model, the Franciscans and Dominicans functioned as itinerant preachers who lived partly in cloister, but also went out of the cloister to preach among the people. By so doing, they provided fresh spiritual energy for the seminally emerging modern bourgeois era of Western Civilization.

---

[30] The ancient peoples of the Americas' First Nations (Native Americans) see all of creation as family, and they celebrate non-human creatures as also our "sisters and brothers."

[31] See Richard E. Rubenstein, ARISTOTLE'S CHILDREN: *How Christians, Muslims, and Jews Rediscovered Ancient Wisdom and Illuminated the Middle Ages* (Harvest Books, 2004).

While some Dominicans and Franciscans played central roles in the repressive Inquisition, Dominicans of the Spanish School of the Catholic University of Salamanca powerfully criticized the brutal injustice of the early modern Spanish *Conquista*. They paved the way, both philosophically and theologically, for the development of a modern democratic polity based on human rights. Most famously, the Dominican Bartolomé de las Casas (1484-1566) became the pioneering prophet in the struggle against the modern slave-system of the Americas.[32] We may therefore rightfully call Las Casas the early 'father' of Modern Catholic Social Teaching.[33]

The Franciscan movement in turn presented a spiritual challenge to two great evils that would become central to later modern bourgeois civilization, namely, *bourgeois greed for money* (resulting in exploitation of God's beloved humans who were poor) and *bourgeois loss of spiritual reverence for Nature* (leading to anti-ecological economic plundering of God's other beloved creatures within the natural world).

In solidarity with the poor, the Latin name of Francis' movement as *Fratres Menores* could be translated as the "Brothers of the Lower Class." This socio-economic interpretation resonates with Jesus' own identification with the poor and the least ones, as well as with contemporary Catholicism's evangelically rooted "preferential option for the poor." In the spirit of that translation, Francis asked his followers to wear the simple and rough clothing of the impoverished lower class.

---

[32] On Las Casas, see the moving study by Gustavo Gutiérrez, LAS CASAS: *In Search of the Poor of Jesus Christ*, trans. Robert R. Barr (Orbis Books, 1993). The original Spanish version is DIOS O EL ORO DE LAS INDIAS (Salamanca: Síguame, 1990). The Spanish title (God or the Gold of the Indies) is more revealing of the book's powerful message. See also Las Casas' own short but powerful work, one among many in his vast corpus of writings about the *Conquista*, THE DEVASTATION OF THE INDIES: *A Brief Account*, trans. Herma Briffault (Johns Hopkins University Press, 1992).

[33] I am indebted to Rev. Stephen Judd MM for this insight.

In addition, Francis' spirituality preserved the *pre-classical ecological-feminine spirituality of divine immanence,* as sacramentally revealed in and through Nature ("Mother Earth"). Francis thus implicitly retrieved the cosmic spirituality of the indigenous Irish-Keltic missionary evangelization and of the early church, and he continued the coenobitical desire to return to the wilderness as a symbolic recovery of the biblical Garden of Eden.

Long before the Irish-Keltic missionary evangelization, Francis' native province of Umbria had been an ancient center of the Keltic tradition's Nature-oriented spirituality. Prior to the imperial Roman conquest, Keltic culture had expanded from today's Turkey across Western Europe to the British Isles, and it included a strong presence in Northern Italy. Thus, in a manner reminiscent of Keltic culture's mystical love of Nature, Francis prayed in song and dance – like Moses' sister Miriam before the Ark of the Covenant – and he embraced both human and non-human creatures as his sisters and brothers.

For these reasons, Francis symbolizes for us today a visionary Catholic spiritual leader who refused to accept the temptation from certain classical and Hellenistic strains to demean material creation. For that reason, Francis stands out still today as a special Catholic saint for the emerging Postmodern Ecological Spirituality.

Some sectors of the later Franciscan movement, however, weakened Francis' radical vision for his movement. For example, as noted, the evangelically challenging name of his movement as *Fratres Menores* has been rendered today in English as the meaningless Latinism "Friars Minor." Similarly, some have converted Francis' embrace of the clothing of the poor into a "religious habit," supposedly separating its wearers from "secular" members of society, and often costing more than the normal clothing of the "secular" middle class.

In addition, as also noted, Francis' original evangelical celebration of an egalitarian lay community became hierarchically classified into "first, second, and third orders," ranked according to the supposed "order" of superiority claimed by Latin patriarchal clericalism. Yet, on a positive note, what became the Franciscan "third order" (today also called "secular Franciscans") did welcome into its core the sacrament of Christian Marriage.

New Bourgeois Universities

Along with the dramatic growth of high-medieval bourgeois wealth, there also developed an explosion of new knowledge carried along the Eastern trading routes and from the African-Muslim kingdom in the south of Spain (*Al-Andalus* or *Andalucía*). Since the narrow limits of monastic libraries could no longer contain the medieval explosion of knowledge, there emerged the important new Western bourgeois institution known today as the *university*. Though initially often governed by cooperative communities of lay scholars, most of these new academic institutions were soon taken over by the new mendicant "religious orders."

Interestingly, there remained an historical connection between the development of those early Western universities and the surviving intellectual influence across continental Europe of the missionary scholars from the great Irish-Keltic monastic schools. For example, Benedict Fitzpatrick linked Thomas Aquinas' recovery of Aristotle to his Irish-Keltic teacher at Naples. Thus, Fitzpatrick reported:

> *Long after the period of the Irish apostolate the fame of Irish learning lingered in Italy, and in the thirteenth century when the Emperor Frederick II founded the University of Naples, he summoned from Ireland and appointed as his first rector Peter Hibernicus, among whose pupils was no less a personage than St. Thomas Aquinas.*

> *Peter was one of a group of Irish literati at the brilliant court of Frederick, where among others resided about the same period*

Michael the Irishman (Scotus), who learnt Arabic at Toledo and was skilled in Hebrew, and who, with Hermann the German and Andreas the Jew, was instrumental in introducing to Europe several of the philosophical works of Aristotle that before that time had remained unknown in the West.[34]

The medieval bourgeois transformation of the knowledge system, beyond the limits of feudal monasticism, inevitably brought a powerful clash between the old monastic culture of knowledge and the mendicant-led university culture. Umberto Eco's famous novel, THE NAME OF THE ROSE, stands as a masterful journey of literary fiction into that profound epistemological and ecclesial transformation, which eventually helped to create Modern Science.[35]

Apostolic Communities Ministering within Modern Capitalism (1500-2000)

The Modern Western Era, emerging in 1500 (rounded-off date), gave birth to the beginnings of Modern Western Industrial-Colonial Civilization. The 'efficiently' organized modern Atlantic slave-system, with its "Triangular Trade" and its early modern stock-markets (reportedly beginning in Antwerp as speculation on profits from slave ships coming there to deposit the profits) constituted first expressions of that new era. Soon, there emerged in England the early modern Factory Revolution, which imitated the 'efficiency' of Caribbean slave plantations, but with 'free labor.' The Factory Revolution later expanded in productivity with industrial mechanization.

Such institutions established the beginnings of Modern Industrial-Colonial Capitalism. From those processes, there also developed across the colonizing countries a militarist-imperialist nationalism,

---

[34] Fitzpatrick, IRELAND AND THE FOUNDATIONS OF EUROPE, p. 336.

[35] Umberto Eco, THE NAME OF THE ROSE (Mariner Books, Reprint Edition, 2014).

along with intertwined industrial exploitation of Nature and the poor. Over the long term, that same process generated a new bourgeois individualism, centered in an anti-ecological, selfishly possessive, and destructively materialistic consumerism.[36]

In spiritual response to the development of this new bourgeois form of Western Civilization, there emerged yet another new form of special Catholic mystical-prophetic intentional communities, the "apostolic" model of "religious life."[37] That new "apostolic" form eventually provided *specialized professional ministries* for the increasingly complex and uprooting bourgeois society, and especially for the millions of uprooted and migrating European peasants who were becoming the modern industrial working class, as well as for missionary evangelization across the new areas of Western imperial colonization.

Professional Apostolates
for Modern Bourgeois Civilization

The naming of new modern Catholic mystical-prophetic intentional communities as the "apostolic" form of "religious life" meant that they provided outside the cloister specialized "apostolates," eventually professional in character and designed to meet the more complex needs of Modern Western Industrial-Colonial Civilization.

The famous prototype of the modern "apostolic" form is the Society of Jesus (Jesuits), founded by the Basque military noble, Ignatius of Loyola (1491-1556). Drawing on the late medieval *Devotio Moderna*,

---

[36] For an insightful investigation of the philosophical development of that process, see the great work of C. B. Macpherson, THE POLITICAL PROCESS OF POLITICAL INDIVIDUALISM: *Hobbes to Locke*, (Oxford University Press Reprint Edition, 2011).

[37] Cada et al., in SHAPING THE COMING AGE OF RELIGIOUS LIFE, divide this period into two sections. They call the first the "Age of the Apostolic Orders" (1500-1800), and the second the "Age of the Teaching Congregations" (1800 ...). Others call the second the age of the missionary orders. In my analysis, however, those two periods constitute two successive phases within the one "Apostolic" model.

Ignatius developed his own model of psychological "Spiritual Exercises." True to the new bourgeois spirituality, these Exercises functioned as *a psychologized monastery,* cultivated within the interior psyche, yet supporting exterior "apostolates" to the 'secular' world.

In addition, the Jesuits provided Catholic shock-troops for the new battles with Protestantism and with the anti-Catholic wing of the rising bourgeoisie. They also established beachheads within Catholic bourgeois families, especially through spiritual direction of elite women and through the secondary education (and later higher education) of their elite children.

Uprooting of the Rural Peasantry

With the rise of industrial modernization in England, bourgeois capitalists began a long-term process of restructuring the countryside by uprooting rural peasants from it. Displaced peasants, desperate for work, migrated to the new industrial towns. In that migration, the uprooted peasants – initially in England and eventually across the planet – lost their communal support system from traditional rural villages. [38] They became the "urban proletariat" or "industrial-working class," living in harsh urban-industrial slums and largely without societal care.

At least within the industrial center-countries, the mainstream of industrial-working class in the industrial-center countries would later achieve the semi-affluent status of "middle class." That would be due to their self-organization into unions, and their political support for creation of the social-welfare state. That semi-affluence would also be

---

[38] On the uprooting of the English peasantry in the early modern English Enclosure Movement, as the first in a series of what Rubenstein calls modern (industrial-linked) "genocides" that included the nineteenth-century Irish Famine (actually an empire-forced starvation), see Richard Rubenstein, THE AGE OF TRIAGE (Beacon Press, 1984).

subsidized, however, by capital flows from the colonial periphery, and by expanding employment for increasing military production.

That semi-affluent status within the industrial center-countries peaked in the middle years of the twentieth century. With the onset of neoliberal industrial globalization (gaining strength in the 1970s), there then began a downwardly mobile process that economically and politically undermined both "blue-collar" and "white-collar" middle classes through neoliberal attacks on unions, foreign "outsourcing" of industrial jobs to regions of "cheap labor," technological "automation," and government policies of "austerity."

Further, the long-term modern bourgeois process of uprooting rural people from their traditional agrarian communities continues today across the globe.[39] For example, as a result of the Western neoliberal capitalist-financial partnership in China's industrialization, the Chinese Communist State has been undertaking what is probably the world's largest ever historical destruction of rural peasant village life.

Blossoming of Women's
"Apostolic" Communities

With the Western onset of modern industrialization and urbanization, the new urban industrial working class lost many of the social functions that *women* had provided within the traditional rural village community: care for the sick, education of the young, sustenance for the poor, provision for the elderly, and charity for the poor. These functions were no longer immediately available within the anonymous, fragmented, and impoverished context of early urban working-class life constructed by hyper-masculine Modern Western Industrial-Colonial Capitalism.

---

[39] See Mike Davis, PLANET OF SLUMS, Reprint Edition (Verso, 2007).

In strategic spiritual response to hyper-masculine industrialization exploding across the late 18th, 19th, and early 20th Centuries, there emerged countless new Catholic mystical-prophetic intentional communities founded by women. These new feminine "apostolic" congregations launched heroic social-service ministries of health, education, and welfare – again, especially for the exploited and impoverished working class of the industrializing countries, as well as for migrating farm families.

In addition, "apostolic" communities of women, as well as of men, provided missionary services within the regions violently conquered by Western Industrial Colonialism, though sometimes without critiquing their supportive role for the colonizing powers, and sometimes even participating in the cruelty of that colonization.

In summary, those "apostolic" communities created what I humorously, but with great admiration, have called the "Catholic Department of Health, Education and Welfare." Their "apostolates" have included schools, hospitals, orphanages, and charitable enterprises. Such "apostolic works" were forerunners of the secular social-welfare state.

Sacrament of Marriage Still Excluded

Yet, as with the earlier forms of "religious life," the core of those "apostolic" communities" did not include the Sacrament of Marriage. Indeed, for a long time in some apostolic orders, those who entered were typically not allowed during their novitiates, and sometimes later as well, to share a meal with their Catholic parents who raised them, or to sleep in their own parents' home. How profound the loss of the original evangelical *Laos*.

The Irish historian John Bossy has claimed that the "clerical" architects of the Catholic Counter-Reformation (out of which the "apostolic" model of "religious life" arose) *deliberately tried to break the organic link between evangelization and the familial kinship system,* even though the kinship system had been the primary and fundamental vehicle of evangelization since the time of Jesus' original apostles.

According to John Bossy, the reason for that attempted break between the modern Western Catholic evangelization and the ancient kinship system was that *the family relatives became a powerful network for Protestant penetration into the Catholic lands.* Within that context, uprooting "apostolic religious" from their biological families of origin, and then training them as uprooted professional evangelizers, served the anti-Protestant goals of the Catholic Counter-Reformation.[40]

Something similar happened with the Catholic Counter-Reformation's creation of the modern seminary system for training candidates to the Catholic presbyterate. It uprooted "seminarians" from the locally rooted kinship system.

By contrast, the Reformation's promise of legalizing the common-law marriages of Catholic presbyters, and of legalizing their (so-called) canonically 'illegitimate' children, presumably became for many Catholic presbyters and their families an attractive feature of the new Protestant movement. At the time, large numbers of European diocesan presbyters maintained common-law marriages with women whom they loved, and they fathered children whom they also loved.

The Protestant Reformation's return to the ancient apostolic tradition of married bishops and presbyters, forcibly suppressed within the Roman Church since the 11th-Century's 'Gregorian Reform,' may in part explain the Reformation's success in Northern Europe. At the time of the Reformation, police-power was no longer available in the

---

[40] See John Bossy, "The Counter Reformation and the People of Catholic Europe," THE PAST AND PRESENT SOCIETY, Number 47 (Oxford University Press, 1970), pages 51-70. I am indebted to Cardinal Francis Stafford for this information, which he shared when, as a young priest, he served as Director of the Family Life Office of the Catholic bishops' conference of the United States.

northern European regions for the papacy to continue suppressing that apostolic tradition.

Late Modern Neoliberal Corporatization

As we have seen, "apostolic religious communities" provided evangelical prototypes for how social-welfare institutions could creatively function in the industrialized center-countries, and in the invaded countries of the colonial or neo-colonial periphery. In recent times, however, at least within the United States, many of these "apostolates" have become *corporatized by lay trustees*, who by and large are capitalist business owners and executives following the neoliberal ideology.

As a result, many Catholic hospitals and universities in the United States now follow the neoliberal corporate-business model. The most obvious example occurs when managers of Catholic hospitals, schools, and charitable enterprises – in violation of Catholic Social Teaching – try to prevent their employees from organizing into a labor union.

During the first half of the twentieth century, Catholic leaders in the United States created close to *two hundred labor schools or union training programs* to educate leaders for the labor movement at every level.[41] Yet today, to my knowledge, the only such schools still existing in the United States are the Labor Guild and Institute of Industrial Relations of the Archdiocese of Boston and the Labor Studies Program at New York City's Manhattan College (a program created by

---

[41] See Rev. Patrick Sullivan, CSC, FIVE GIANTS IN THE BISHOP'S SOCIAL ACTION DEPARTMENT AMONG MORE THAN FOUR HUNDRED U.S. CATHOLIC LABOR PRIESTS (Pacem in Terris Press, 2014), Volume One in the series titled CATHOLIC LABOR PRIESTS IN THE UNITED STATES: *A 20th Century Story of Solidarity*.

Dr. Joseph Fahey, founding chairperson of Catholic Scholars for Worker Justice).[42]

In place of those two-hundred labor schools, Catholic educational leaders in the United States have established at Catholic colleges and universities close to *two hundred business schools or business training programs.* We might describe this strategic class-shift from approximately two-hundred labor schools to approximately two hundred business schools as the "bourgeois captivity" of so many leaders of American-Catholic higher education.[43]

Again, even though many "apostolic religious communities" once sought to serve the *industrial working class,* some current leaders of "religious apostolates" now follow the *anti-worker prejudice* of the neoliberal corporate business class that fills the boards of trustees of their hospitals and universities. That reality reveals a sad institutional loss of prophetic spirituality.

Historical Decline of Modern Apostolic Religious Communities

The modern period of dominance for the "apostolic" model of "religious life" lasted approximately from 1500 to 2000 (again, rounded-off to centuries). At least for the 'advanced' industrial countries, we now see the sunset of the "apostolic" model of Catholic mystical-prophetic intentional communities, which the Holy Spirit had prophetically inspired to address the societal challenges emerging from the rise of Modern Western Industrial-Colonial Civilization.

In a similar manner across earlier forms of Western Civilization, earlier periods of Western church history saw the sunset of their

---

[42] For information on the Labor Guild, see *http://laborguild.com,* and for information on Catholic Scholars for Worker Justice, see *http:cswj.us* (both accessed 2017-04-30).

[43] See Chapters 1 and 7 of Joe Holland, 100 YEARS OF CATHOLIC SOCIAL TEACHING DEFENDING WORKERS AND THEIR UNIONS (Pacem in Terris Press, 2012).

dominant spiritual model – of the mendicant model for medieval bourgeois society, of the monastic model for feudal-aristocratic society, of the coenobitical model for late classical imperial society, and even of the foundational lay model with its messianic spiritual challenge to the idolatrous and oppressive Roman Empire. All these models long ago entered their historical decline.

In ending this chapter, let us recall that we have seen how the late modern form of Modern Industrial Civilization is precipitating a breakdown of integral ecology throughout its interwoven natural, human, and spiritual fabric, across our loving Creator's beloved garden-planet Earth. That is happening even as the late modern neoliberal global expression of Liberal Capitalism appears to triumph technologically and ideologically. Yet visionary pioneers are already planting creative seeds for an alternative Postmodern Ecological Civilization.

Understanding the emerging Postmodern Ecological Era with its new historical challenge for human spirituality, and within it for Catholic spirituality, becomes essential for discerning the vocation, identity, and mission of the emerging postmodern *lay form* of Catholic mystical-prophetic intentional communities. It also becomes essential for discerning what *revised role* modern Catholic "apostolic religious communities" seeking "refounding" might play in the emerging Postmodern Era, as well as for discerning how to develop a postmodern "New Evangelization" that will draw on the emerging Postmodern Ecological Spirituality.

This chapter has reviewed the first five stages of what this book calls Catholic mystical-prophetic intentional communities. The next two chapters will explore the late modern breakdown of Modern Psychological Spirituality, which arose in correlation with the rise of Modern Industrial Civilization. It was that receding spirituality, in Catholic form, that provided the spiritual grounding for the modern, and yet now receding, "apostolic" form of "religious life."

3

NEW LAY WAVE OF

POSTMODERN ECOLOGICAL SPIRITUALITY

This chapter explores the emergence and nature of Postmodern Ecological Spirituality. This Postmodern Ecological Spirituality has both new and old dimensions within human consciousness.

Old & New Dimensions of
Ecological Spirituality

We find *ancient yet still living human roots* for ecological spirituality in the Nature-grounded traditions of Indigenous Peoples across our garden-planet Earth. These rich eco-spiritual traditions help all of us to recall the ancient eco-spiritual tribal traditions from which we are all descended.

We also find *ancient yet still living biblical roots* for this spirituality in the cosmic spirituality of thanksgiving and praise within the Hebrew Scriptures, especially the Psalms, and in the Christian New Testament's proclamation of cosmic salvation. In addition, we find *ancient yet still living Catholic roots* in the sacramental understanding of creation, which is also found within Orthodox and Anglican Christianity.

The new dimension of Postmodern Ecological Spirituality is of course not found in those ancient roots, but rather in the still developing scientific discovery of *cosmic evolution*, including the evolution of life on our garden-planet Earth, and within it of our own human family's reflective consciousness.

Yet, for the emerging ecological spirituality, evolution is not understood though the atomistic-mechanical reductionism of modern Scientific-Materialism, which has cosmologically grounded Darwinian and Neo-Darwinian interpretations of evolution. Rather, it is found in the holistic and post-Darwinian understanding of evolution being explored by visionary scientists like Fritjof Capra and Pier Luigi Luisi,[1] as well as by mystical-prophetic figures like the late eco-spiritual visionary Thomas Berry.[2]

Further, Postmodern Ecological Spirituality finds its grounding in mystical-prophetic consciousness of the Divine Mystery present both within and beyond creation. It finds that grounding in the mystical dimension of the evolutionary creative communion unfolding across our splendorous Cosmos, across our beauteous garden-planet Earth, across Earth's vibrant biosphere of which we are part, and within our own human family's profound reflective consciousness.

What is new in this mystical-prophetic awakening is that all created reality has evolved and is still evolving. Further, in this awakening, postmodern Christians discover that cosmic creatures are not *passive objects* of our Creator's loving creativity, but *profoundly active co-creators* with our loving Creator's own divine creativity. Hence, Postmodern Global Ecological Spirituality constitutes a spirituality of *ecological co-creativity*, or alternately of *creative communion*.

---

[1] See their pioneering book, THE SYSTEMS VIEW OF LIFE: *A Unifying Vision* (Cambridge University Press, 2014).

[2] See, for example, one of his last major books, THE GREAT WORK: *Our Way into the Future* (Three Rivers Press / Crown / Random House, 1999).

This *sacred co-creativity* is still holistically revealing its unfolding energy throughout the interwoven natural, human, and spiritual fabric of life's integral ecology across our garden-planet Earth and across our majestic Cosmos. Yet, on the negative side, we have also come to realize that, within this evolving evolutionary-ecological framework, *human sin* has emerged as a blasphemous and death-dealing attack on the creative communion of life's integral ecology.

In addition, as we have seen, the Catholic form of this still emerging Postmodern Ecological Spirituality is explicitly *lay*. It roots Catholic spirituality back not only into our loving Creator's wondrous creation of Nature, but also into the foundational lay nature of Christian discipleship. Supporting this lay rootedness, recent scholarship has re-emphasized Jesus' own Jewish identity as lay, and the lay character of the entire early Jesus movement.[3]

As pointed out earlier in this book, Jesus' preaching holistically proclaimed the resurrection of the body and the eschatological renewal of the "Heavens" and Earth. Jesus' holistic proclamation of a Nature-rooted spirituality stands as profoundly opposed to the modern Western drive philosophically and scientifically to de-spiritualize Nature, and technologically and economically to devastate its ecological regeneration.

Ecological Spirituality as Panentheistic

The emerging Postmodern Ecological Spirituality may be described as a form of "*Panentheism*."[4] From its Greek roots, that word means

---

[3] On Jesus as a layperson, see John P. Meyer, A MARGINAL JEW: *Rethinking the Historical Jesus, The Roots of the Problem*, Volume I (Doubleday, 1991).

[4] For more on Panentheism, see the article on the topic in the STANFORD ENCYCLOPEDIA OF PHILOSOPHY at *http://plato.stanford.edu/entries/panentheism* (accessed 2016-09-11). As that article notes, Panentheism finds strong resonances in Eastern Christian Theology. For pioneering Catholic philosophical work in this area, see the article's references to Joseph A. Bracken, SJ. For pioneering Protestant-Christian philosophical work in this area, see the article's references to John Cobb and David Ray Griffin.

"God is in everything" – with "*Pan*" meaning "all," *en*" meaning "in," and "*Theos*" meaning "God," and thus all together meaning "God in all."

Panentheism differs from *Pantheism*, which identifies the Divine Mystery with creation. By contrast, Panentheism perceives the Divine Mystery both as immanently revealed within the depth of creation and as transcending all created reality. Panentheism may also be contrasted with a *purely transcendent Theism*, which perceives the Divine Mystery as revealed only beyond creation, and with a *purely immanent Materialism*, which claims there is no transcendence.

As we have seen earlier, the modern Western bourgeois project tried initially and schizophrenically to combine a purely transcendent Theism for a psychologized spiritual consciousness with a purely immanent Materialism for a reductionist philosophical-scientific understanding of the Universe. Over time, as we have also seen, such a weak psychologized bourgeois spirituality became first privatized, then secularized, and finally nihilized.

In the contemporary late modern period, that intellectual-spiritual degeneration has resulted in a triumphant culture of Scientific Materialism and even Nietzschean Nihilism. As a result, the dominant public values promoted by the materialist-nihilist culture of the corporate global culture industries are now *money, power, and fame*. Hence, the urgent historical need for Postmodern Ecological Spirituality.

Visionary Projects of Ecological Spirituality

Gratefully, we are discovering within contemporary Catholic-Christianity (and elsewhere as well) hope-filled projects rooted in Postmodern Ecological Spirituality. For example, within the United States, we see pioneering members of the Catholic Worker Movement pursuing the agroecological vision of Peter Maurin. They are returning to the land to embrace a rurally rooted way of life that seeks regeneration for the creative communion of life's integral ecology.[5]

Also, some members of Catholic "religious orders," and especially women, have also become visionary pioneers in this emerging Post-modern Ecological Spirituality. One U.S. example is the wonderful work of Sister Miriam Therese MacGillis of the Dominican Sisters of Caldwell. Following the ecological teachings of Thomas Berry, Sister MacGillis has created and sustained the northern New Jersey ecological complex called Genesis Farm.[6] Another example is the ecological reserve known as Maryknoll Ecological Sanctuary, established in the Philippines by the Maryknoll Sisters and originally directed by Maryknoll Sister Ann Braudis.[7]

In addition, there are important Protestant-initiated examples. One creative U.S. example is the visionary project known as the Narrow Ridge Earth Literacy Center in the U.S. State of Tennessee. Grounded in the cosmological vision of Thomas Berry, it was founded by United Methodist minister Bill Nickle, in cooperation with United Methodist lay leader Dr. Macgregor Smith. Today, it is directed by Dr. Mitzi Wood-von Misener.

Celebrating in 2016 its twenty-fifth anniversary, the Narrow Ridge project has developed an ecological village that protects and cherishes more than seven hundred acres of gently rolling Appalachian hills. Encompassing lush green meadows and dark verdant forests, it provides a common ecological home for humans and myriad other creatures, who all live together there within Nature's vibrant family of life.[8]

---

[5] See Eric Anglada, "The History and New Growth of Catholic Worker Farms," AMERICA MAGAZINE, May 6, 2013, available at: *http://americamagazine.org/issue/taking-root*.

[6] See *http://www.genesisfarm.org*.

[7] See *https://maryknollsisters.org/mk-sister/sister-ann-braudis*.

[8] See *http://www.earthliteracycenter.org/about*.

Late Modern Spiritual Erosion

Encouraged by such mystical-prophetic seeds of regeneration, Western Catholic Christianity, and indeed all of global Christianity, is beginning to face the historically new strategic challenge arising from the vast late modern devastation of life's integral ecology. Again, the late modern and now globalized form of Modern Industrial Civilization is the source of that devastation.

At the same time, Western Christians are beginning to face the correlative strategic challenge arising from the breakdown of the West's Modern Psychological Spirituality. That Western bourgeois spirituality – schizophrenically dualist in character – has been undermined by the privatization of religion and by the secularization of society, and it is now collapsing into Nietzschean Nihilism.

As the correlative breakdowns of the late modern Western bourgeois forms of both civilization and spirituality become clear, we find ourselves living today not only in a confusing and turbulent time, but also in a time of great danger. The reason for the danger is that so many late modern institutional leaders are still relentlessly (albeit often unknowingly) promoting the degenerative philosophical paths of Scientific Materialism and even Nietzschean Nihilism. Across our loving Creator's beloved planet Earth, those late modern institutional paths are inflicting vast planetary devastation on life's integral ecology.

Further, as we have also seen for the current late modern period, Western Catholic Christians are experiencing the breakdown of the modern industrial model of evangelization. Within that breakdown of evangelization, they are also experiencing correlative breakdowns of the modern "apostolic" model of "religious life," and of the modern "clerical"-celibate-seminary model of the presbyterate.

Those interrelated but collapsing modern Western Catholic models – for spirituality, for evangelization, for "religious life," and for the presbyterate – were developed within and for the historical context of Modern Western Industrial-Colonial Civilization. They all now face historical breakdown within the wider contextual breakdown of Modern Industrial Civilization.

Restoration, Modernization, or Regeneration?

The solution to the late modern Western Catholic breakdown is not the so-called 'conservative' Christian temptation to *restore* classical cultural-spiritual forms, nor the so-called 'progressive' (or liberal) temptation to *integrate* further with Modernity's collapsing culture.

The "Modern World" (Modern Industrial-Colonial Civilization) has been breaking down for some time.[9] Within that breakdown, any 'progressive' attempt to pursue deeper modernization often becomes pathological. In addition, the late modern breakdown has older roots in the classical cultural-spiritual forms that many 'conservatives' are attempting to restore. For that reason, such 'conservative' attempts can also become spiritually pathological.

Within the terminal crisis of Modernity, many 'conservative' Christians seek (again, in the name of "restoration") to preserve or to recover certain late classical or early modern cultural additions to Christianity. However, many such cultural additions find little or no support from the New Testament. For example, as we have seen for Catholic Christianity, neither the canonical "clerical state in life" nor the canonical "religious state in life" existed in Christianity's foundational and early stages, during which time the Christian movement was entirely lay.

---

[9] For an early and prophetic realization of this breakdown, see the landmark book by the distinguished Italian-German Catholic philosopher Romano Guardini, THE END OF THE MODERN WORLD, Reprint Edition (ISI Books, 1998). Pope Francis, who as a young Jesuit had done graduate studies on Guardini's thought, cited the original German edition of Guardini's book, DAS ENDE DER NEUZEIT, eight times!

Yet, authentic cultural-spiritual gifts of the past – spanning the Primal, Classical, and now receding Modern Eras – all remain valuable, and need to be integrated within the emerging Postmodern Era. To seek a postmodern future that will include authentic cultural-spiritual gifts from all past human eras, we need to allow the inspiring wisdom of the Holy Spirit to guide us in creating a life-giving synthesis. Again, that synthesis needs authentically to conserve past gifts and authentically to progress toward future possibilities.

Once again, as Modern Industrial Civilization and Modern Psychological Spirituality together go deeper and deeper into their late modern breakdowns, we are seeing a correlative decline in the modern Western Catholic industrial model of evangelization. At the same time, we are also seeing correlative declines in the modern Western Catholic "apostolic" model of special mystical-prophetic intentional communities, and in the modern seminary-trained and clerical-celibate model of the Western Catholic presbyterate, at least within the 'advanced' industrial regions.

Within the sad turbulence and confusion of those declines, and for some religious institutions even death, we need to trust that at times of cultural and spiritual chaos, when everything seems to be falling apart, at such times the Holy Spirit seeks to guide us toward the birthing of a new era of spiritual and societal creativity.

Within the depressing and growing *spiritual emptiness* across the late modern industrialized world, prophetic visionaries are returning to the Spirit-inspired dark mystical womb of regeneration. In that mystical darkness, the human experience becomes prophetically regenerated. It then brings forth *freshly creative spiritual energy*. For this reason, Catholic Christianity is now experiencing the global emergence of new lay forms of special Catholic mystical-prophetic intentional communities.

Drinking from Life-Giving
Spiritual Waters

As we have seen, the Christian Church, as the lay gathering of Jesus' disciples, is called to drink from the life-giving waters of the Holy Spirit in order to heal, and to sanctify more deeply, the Creator's beloved, mystical, and yet also sinfully wounded, creation. In addition, as we have seen, the Holy Spirit's regenerative power of healing and deeper sanctification takes distinct historical forms.

Again, Catholic mystical-prophetic intentional communities need to drink deeply from the Holy Spirit's regenerative waters. In relation to that need, two earlier-mentioned points seem worth repeating.

- *Ecclesial Mission.* First, special Catholic mystical-prophetic communities are called to help in healing sinful woundedness within the wider gathering of disciples (that is, to assist in renewing the church's internal life), in order that a renewed church may help to renew the creative communion of life's integral ecology across the wider sin-wounded world.

- *Societal Correlation.* Second, there is always an historical correlation between the historical form of society's woundedness from sin and the historical form of Catholic mystical-prophetic communities arising to renew the church for healing in the sin-wounded world. Thus, as the historical form of society's sin-filled woundedness shifts, so too we experience an historical shift in the deep historical mission of Catholic mystical-prophetic communities.

As we have seen, with the birth of a new era, a form of Catholic mystical-prophetic intentional community that flourished in one historical era goes into decline and a fresh form emerges to occupy its space. But the new era need not eliminate the declining form, for that form can continue as a secondary yet still important part of the church's vast treasury of spiritual energy. The old form may thus play a continuing, albeit reduced, role in the future. In addition, with each new wave of transformation, the wider community of disciples learns new things from both old and new special Catholic mystical-prophetic intentional communities. Yet leadership belongs to the new form.

Like a Flowing River
Suddenly Changing Course

We may think of a spiritual river flowing through an historical valley between two large mountains. Over centuries, the spiritual river had carved in the valley a deep channel flowing with the historical era's spiritual waters of regenerative and co-creative life. Suddenly, an earthquake causes a landslide to tumble down from the mountains. It blocks the river's channel. Quickly, the flowing waters of spiritual life back up behind the blockage.

Before long, however, the backed-up spiritual waters break through into another channel and again flow down into the valley. The newly flowing river of spiritual energy then begins to carve out a new and deepening spiritual channel. Soon, the living waters of spiritual energy flow powerfully down the new channel, while only a small stream continues to slip through the blocked old spiritual channel.

In the wake of the postmodern spiritual earthquake, some wish to dig out again the old blocked channel, and to force a strong flow of spiritual waters back into that old route. Yet that goal proves an impossible quest. The rubble from the historical landslide is too vast. For that reason, it is better to celebrate the new channel of life-giving spiritual waters, to drink deeply from their new course of mystical-prophetic flow, and to rejoice in the regenerative healing of those waters' spiritual strength.

Even so, and again, some spiritual water will continue to flow through the old channel. The flow of spiritual water in the older channel becomes quieter, yet its special healing grace remains. Such is the manner of transformation for the historical-cultural form of special Catholic mystical-prophetic intentional communities within the post-modern spiritual transformation.

In terms of today, the landslide is the postmodern transition, precip-itated by the technological earthquake of the Electronic Revolution. That earthquake has led to the still unfolding breakdown of the mod-ern bourgeois and industrial-colonial form of Western Civilization, including its recent globalization, and for both of its materialist ideo-logies of Liberal Capitalism and Scientific Socialism. Correlatively, it has also led to the contemporary breakdown of the modern bour-geois form of the dualist spirituality of psychological interiority.

Beyond Religious Dualism

As the old modern spiritual channel shrinks, and in some places even dries up, the late modern Western Catholic Church experiences within the industrial-center countries a "vocation crisis" for the mod-ern "apostolic" form of "religious life," which has been grounded in the now collapsing Modern Psychological Spirituality. That modern Western form had once responded powerfully and creatively to the spiritual challenges of the Modern Era. Now, however, within the in-dustrial-center nations that form has fallen into decline.

Yet, the Holy Spirit's life-giving spiritual waters are already spread-ing beyond the old blocked modern channel. They are breaking through to create a new and regenerative postmodern spiritual chan-nel. For that reason, we now see emerging *new lay forms* of Catholic mystical-prophetic intentional communities.

Again, the "apostolic" cultural-spiritual model of "religious life" within the Western Catholic Church was developed for the "Modern World" of the Western industrializing and colonizing nations. Now, it is yielding to the emergence of a postmodern lay spirituality, which this book proposes is called to become ecologically regenerative.

Again, the same shortage of "vocations" for "religious life" is also true for the modern bourgeois seminary-trained and clericalized-celibate model of the Western Catholic presbyterate.

At the Ecumenical Council of Trent (1545-1563), that modern Western model was consolidated in a manner analogous to "religious life." A decree from the Fifth Session of the Council of Trent required special schools for standardized training of future priests. Soon called "seminaries," these schools imitated monastic life. In addition, following the Council of Trent, the monastic-inspired papal law of celibacy was promoted even more intensely by Western Catholic bishops.[10] Thus, the modern Western Catholic model of the presbyter-ate was constructed in three historical stages.

- *Stage 1 - Imperial Clericalism.* In the fourth century, the Emperor Constantine legally 'elevated' bishops and presbyters to a 'higher' imperial class authorized to rule over the "laity," with laity then demoted below the "clergy" in the hierarchical structure of the new Imperial Church.

- *Stage 2 - Monastic Celibacy.* In the eleventh century, the papal 'Gregorian Reform,' inspired by the monastic network of Cluny, violently imposed monastic celibacy by police force on the then

---

[10] As we saw in Chapter 2, in the fourth century the Catholic episcopacy and presbyterate had been clericalized by the Roman Empire's Constantinian construction of the Imperial Church. Much later, in the eleventh century, the 'Gregorian Reform' had imported its papal law of celibacy from monasticism and imposed it by police-force on the largely married Western Catholic diocesan presbyters and bishops. As also noted earlier, that monastic-inspired papal campaign was in part justified by misogynist contempt for women, and it even involved papal enslavement of presbyters' wives and children. But the deep motive seems to have been papal lust for theocratic power. Yet common-law clerical marriages continued across the West long after the so-called 'Gregorian Reform,' and long after the Council of Trent, especially in rural regions.

largely married Western diocesan bishops and presbyters, in order to support a new papal theocracy.

- *Stage 3 - Monastic Seminaries.* In the sixteenth century, the Council of Trent decreed that candidates for the diocesan presbyterate should be trained outside universities and in ecclesial segregation from the rest of the priestly *Laos*. The purpose of his segregation was to combat Protestantism's penetration into kinship networks within Catholic regions. This segregation uprooted Catholic evangelization from its traditional roots, dating back to apostolic times, in locally rooted kinship and friendship networks.

The Protestant Reformation rightfully rejected the non-evangelical papal law of monastic celibacy for Western diocesan presbyters and bishops, and it successfully launched its long and still continuing wave of evangelization. The Reformation's rejection of that papal law may have been one of the major reasons for the Reformation's initial successes in Northern Europe. It may also be one of the major reasons for the still growing success in evangelization of Protestant Evangelical and Pentecostal movements throughout the world.

Further, outside Western Catholic Christianity, practically all of the other twenty-three *sui juris* Churches of the global Catholic communion never accepted monastic celibacy as mandatory law for diocesan presbyters. They still largely follow the ancient apostolic tradition of allowing married presbyters, if not bishops. Finally, the non-evangelical papal law of monastic celibacy for diocesan presbyters never existed as a broad institutional policy within the Western Church during its entire first millennium.

Today, the modern clerical-celibate-seminary model for Catholic presbyters in the Western Church is breaking down. That breakdown is revealed through the "shortage of vocations" and through the often intellectually weak and sometimes emotionally unhealthy quality of seminarians.[11]

But most of the contemporary Western Catholic bishops still resist understanding the depth of this historical-spiritual breakdown of the modern Western Catholic clerical-celibate-seminary model of the presbyterate.[12] They also still resist understanding the relationship of that historical-spiritual breakdown to the wider historical-spiritual breakdown of Catholic evangelization across the Western industrial-center countries. Again, those breakdowns form part of the wider and correlative Western breakdowns of Modern Psychological Spirituality and of Modern Industrial Civilization.

At the end of the aristocratic *Ancien Régime,* the Western European Catholic episcopacy remained imprisoned in what might be called its "aristocratic captivity." It failed to understand the deep spiritual challenges emerging from the Industrial Revolution. In major regions of Western Europe, that failure caused the massive failure of evangelization called the "loss of the working class."

Today, across the industrial center countries of Western Civilization, we see what might now be called the Western Catholic episcopacy's "bourgeois captivity." Often enmeshed in a corporate-capitalist model of leadership, many bishops remain blind to the deep spiritual challenges emerging from the Electronic Revolution. As a result, yet

---

[11] For a reflection on this breakdown, see the essay by Alberto Melloni, *"La messa è finita. Così dopo cinque secoli tramonta la figura del prete,"* LA REPUBBLICA (Italy), 2017-03-22, available at *http://ilsismografo.blogspot.it/2017/03/italia-la-messa-e-finita.html* (accessed 2017-03-30). For an English-language article on this essay see Robert Mickens, "Letter from Rome: The Church's Seminary Problem," COMMONWEAL MAGAZINE, 2017-03-27, available at *https://www.commonwealmagazine.org/letter-rome-117* (accessed 2017-03-30).

[12] Despite the crisis of "vocations" for the clerical-celibate-seminary model of the presbyterate, there seems to be a surplus of Western Catholic presbyters pursuing a "vocation" to the episcopate. That may be due due to the sociological disease of careerism found in all human institutions.

another great Western de-evangelization is now occurring, and this time especially across the 'advanced' English-speaking countries of Modern Industrial Civilization.

Yet there is no shortage of "vocations" for ordained ministerial leadership within the Protestant Reformation's contemporary Evangelical and Pentecostal movements.[13] The reason is that those still growing Christian movements have rejected for ministerial leadership the non-evangelical model of clericalism, as well as the non-evangelical requirement of celibacy. In their place, they have embraced the *original lay form of ecclesial leadership*. In addition, many of those pastoral leaders have embraced the Electronic Revolution as a central medium for evangelization.

More importantly, the still globally expanding Evangelical and Pentecostal movements have returned to the ancient Christian tradition of pursuing evangelization, and of discerning ecclesial leadership within evangelization, primarily through *locally-rooted lay kinship and friendship networks.* In that return, Evangelical and Pentecostal movements frequently ordain local grass-roots leaders and often allow them to stay and to minister within their local communities, as happened in the original lay movement of Jesus' disciples.

Those contemporary Reformation movements have thus rejected the deracinated and segregated clerical-celibate-seminary model for ordained leadership developed by the Catholic papacy in the late classical, medieval and modern periods. They have also often rejected the deracinated professionalized model developed for the "mainline"

---

[13] These churches are different from the "mainline" Protestant denominations, which have maintained a deracinated professionalism for ministerial leadership. Further, the "mainlines" have by and large become culturally accommodated to Modernity, and thus often lack the counter-cultural spiritual energy found in the Evangelical and Pentecostal movements. But the "mainline" Protestant churches, at least in the United States, have a different problem. While they do not have a shortage of "vocations" for pastoral ministry, they do have a growing shortage of congregational members to serve.

Protestant Churches, which sought cultural integration with Modern Philosophy and Modern Science as the intellectual foundations for Modern Industrial Civilization.

Consequently, across the globe, Evangelical and Pentecostal movements, and especially Pentecostal movements which empower grass-roots women, have been dramatically expanding their evangelization. Meanwhile, within the 'advanced' industrial-center countries, the uprooted and segregated clerical-celibate-seminary model of the Catholic presbyterate collapses into ever deeper crisis, and at times in a pathological manner.

Thus, the late modern crisis of the Western Catholic presbyterate within the industrial center-countries remains inseparable from the Western Church's non-evangelical law of celibacy for diocesan presbyters and bishops. Yet changing that papal law will not of itself resolve the late modern crisis of Catholic evangelization, though such a change is surely a necessary pre-condition. To address the crisis at the deep level, however, there will also need to be a profound transformation in the grounding spirituality, as well as a return to the apostolic model of ordaining local grass-roots leaders to the presbyterate without the clerical-celibate-seminary superstructure.

Of course, voluntary evangelical celibacy constitutes an important spiritual charism for those whom the Holy Spirit calls to it. But human-made church law cannot forcibly impose the Holy Spirit's gift of a special charism on an institutional office. When that happens, there eventually occurs an anti-spiritual distortion of the very nature of that office, as well as an institutional weakening of its spiritual power.

Further, as we have seen, the postmodern cultural-spiritual transformation, in its *deep mythic-symbolic foundation,* is moving beyond classical hierarchical patriarchy and beyond modern hyper-masculinism (with both carrying undertows of misogyny), and toward an egalitarian and co-creative partnership of feminine and masculine spiritual energy. For that reason, it is now essential to create across global Catholic Christianity *regenerative postmodern paths empowering women's spiritual leadership.*

Deep Mission of Postmodern Lay
Ecological Communities

The new historical-cultural context is the deep transition from the now globalized form of Modern Industrial Civilization toward the future global emergence of a Postmodern Ecological Civilization. In addition, as we have seen, correlated with this deep societal transition is the *deep spiritual transition* from Modern Psychological Spirituality which has been Western and dualistic, toward Postmodern Ecological Spirituality which is global and holistic.

Within this transitional framework, we have also seen that there is emerging a fresh Catholic spiritual wave of *postmodern lay movements.* Again, these movements intentional are the newest historical form of special Catholic mystical-prophetic communities. This new wave follows the past waves of foundational, coenobitical, monastic, mendicant, and apostolic communities. Like those earlier waves, this new one responds to a new historical context. Thus, while the modern Western "apostolic "form of Catholic mystical-prophetic communities has been declining within the 'advanced' industrial countries, these new postmodern lay movements have been growing.

New Mission of Ecological Regeneration

Within this postmodern societal-spiritual transformation, what needs to become the *deep spiritual mission* of this postmodern lay wave of special Catholic mystical-prophetic intentional communities?

- *Classical Restoration.* Is it to *restore* the elitist and dualistic Platonic spirituality of late classical aristocratic and hierarchical-patriarchal culture?

- *Modern Integration.* Is it to *integrate* further with the now disintegrating atomistic-mechanical and materialist culture of hyper-masculine bourgeois Modernity, which has secularized Nature and society and both privatized and undermined religion?

- *Postmodern Regeneration.* Or is the mission to *regenerate* our loving Creator's evolving integral ecology of life, within a fresh postmodern framework that is holistic and global, while remaining faithfully rooted in authentic ancient Christian traditions?

If the deep spiritual mission is indeed holistic postmodern regeneration of life's integral ecology, then how should that mission be described? Again, I have proposed that the deep historical mission for the postmodern wave of new Catholic lay movements may be described as follows:

> *The Holy Spirit is now calling us both personally and institutionally to embody and to preach the Good News of Jesus in and through holistic regeneration of the evolving creative communion of life's integral ecology, throughout its interwoven natural, human, and spiritual fabric, and across our loving Creator's beloved garden-planet Earth.*

This needs to become the *deep spiritual mission* not only for special Catholic mystical-prophetic intentional communities, but also for the wider global communion of Catholic Christian Churches, and indeed for the entire global Christian family. Further, this deep spiritual mission needs to undergird the existing missions of all contemporary institutions within global Christianity.

Retrieving the
Regenerative Lay Model of Church

As expressly lay in identity, the new Catholic movements typically welcome women and men, celibates and marrieds, and children too. In so doing, they move beyond the mono-sexual celibate monopoly that has characterized earlier historical-cultural models for Catholic mystical-prophetic intentional communities.

By embracing women and men, marrieds and singles, and children as well, these new lay movements are returning to the *foundational lay model of the early Jesus' movement*. They are allowing the Holy Spirit to re-root their evangelical-sacramental energy back into the original spiritual power of Jesus' foundational *Laos*.

Further, by virtue of their lay character, these communities implicitly do not follow the *world-rejecting spirituality* of many earlier forms of Catholic mystical-prophetic intentional communities. As we have seen, much of the earlier tradition of Catholic "religious life" carried, along with its evangelical-sacramental richness, an anti-worldly legacy known in Latin as the *fuga mundi* (flight from the world). Even modern "apostolic" communities, despite magnanimously serving the "secular world" through their outer-directed "apostolates," nonetheless attempted in their inner-directed psychological spirituality of interiority to "retreat" from the world.

By contrast, postmodern Catholic lay movements, again by virtue of their self-consciousness lay character, are implicitly following a *world-affirming spirituality*. While modern "apostolic" communities have understood themselves as separate from the "secular world," postmodern lay communities find their identity and mission within their lay character and within the so-called "secular world."

Further, through their lay identity, postmodern Catholic lay movements are rediscovering the foundational nature of the lay baptismal path to holiness within the sacred realities of *family, work, and citizenship.* These realities are indeed sacred, because they co-creatively share in our loving Creator's own Divine Creativity. Many emerging postmodern lay movements have rooted their charisms in at least one of these three sacred human areas of the creative communion of life. Again, these are family, work, and citizenship. That is where their charism of lay spirituality takes practical root.

Contemporary examples of these lay movements include multiple new creations. Movements favored by Catholic popes in the late twentieth century have tended to be so-called 'conservative' in character, yet they embrace a world-affirming spirituality. One such example is Opus Dei, which roots its spirituality in the sacred task of *human work.* Additional examples include communities of the Charismatic Renewal and Focolare, both of which stress the sacred task of *family.* Still another example is Communion and Liberation, which emphasizes Christian education for societal life, which we might describe as linked to the sacred task of *citizenship.*

There are also so-called 'progressive' lay movements like the Catholic Worker, L'Arche, the Jesuit-linked Christian Life Communities, Maryknoll Lay Missionaries and Affiliates, Pax Christi, Pax Romana, San Egidio, 'Secular' Franciscans, etc. Many of these 'progressive' movements stress the post-Vatican II themes of "justice and peace," and many have recently added the theme of ecology. By and large, we may interpret these 'progressive' emphases as related to the sacred lay task of *citizenship.* These 'progressive' movements seem weaker, however, in their spiritual celebration of the sacred character of family and work.

Beyond Deficiencies,
One-Sidedness, & Polarization

Historically, new movements of Catholic mystical-prophetic intentional communities have in their initial forms often carried deficiencies.

For example, Saint Francis of Assisi did not invent the medieval Italian model of devotion to the poor by becoming poor Catholic beggars (mendicants). During Francis' time, there had already been formed within Italy diverse bands of Christian beggars known as the *poverelli* (the poor ones). Reportedly, however, some of them had the unfortunate practice of assassinating Western Catholic bishops addicted to aristocratic opulence and power. Francis purified that already existing mendicant model by promoting non-violence and peace. His purified peaceful model then flourished, while the violent model did not.

A late modern deficiency appears within some contemporary Catholic lay movements when their leaders pursue only a one-sided 'conservative' strategy of premodern *restoration*, or a one-sided 'progressive' strategy of modern *integration*, rather than a holistic ecological strategy of postmodern *regeneration*.[14]

When that happens, such leaders become partially trapped in one or the other poles of the *tragic late modern polarization*. They become at least partially trapped either within the reactionary late-modern restoration strategy, or within the disintegrating late-modern integration strategy. When that happens, members at both dysfunctional poles can easily slide into fear, resentment, and even hatred toward those following the other partially dysfunctional pole. Such bitter polarization then becomes the opposite of Jesus' call to unity in love.

Further, there is also a problem in the way that many new postmodern lay movements celebrate the sacred lay spiritual co-creativity expressed through family, work, and citizenship. In so doing, they rightfully become counter-cultural in relation to the collapsing late modern bourgeois model of civilization. Yet they often become

---

[14] For an earlier and preliminary exploration of these three strategies of restoration, modernization, and regeneration, see Anne Barsanti & Joe Holland, AMERICAN AND CATHOLIC: *The New Debate* (Pillar Books, 1987).

counter-cultural only in a one-sided manner. While counter-cultur-ally criticizing one pole of degenerative late-modern bourgeois con-sciousness, they can remain imprisoned within its opposite pole.

Thus, for Western Catholic movements on the so-called 'conservative' side, their counter-cultural spiritual energy appears typically de-voted to challenging the psychologically oriented *expressive individu-alism* of late modern bourgeois culture, and especially in the psycho-sexual area. This 'conservative' side criticizes what Robert Bellah and his colleagues, in their sociological classic HABITS OF THE HEART, have called Modernity's "*therapeutic ethos.*"[15]

Meanwhile, for Western Catholic movements on the 'progressive' side, their counter-cultural energy appears typically devoted to chal-lenging the technologically oriented *instrumental individualism* of the late modern bourgeois political economy. This 'progressive' side crit-icizes what Robert Bellah and his colleagues in HABITS OF THE HEART have called Modernity's "*managerial ethos.*"

As a result, across Western Catholic Christianity, these 'conservative' and 'progressive' one-sided limitations often prevent Catholic lay movements from becoming fully postmodern, and from fully serving the regeneration of life's integral ecology.

In rejecting bourgeois Modernity's psychologically oriented expres-sive individualism, the late modern 'conservative' wing emphasizes subordination of the psychological self to disciplined institutional structures and traditions. It is therefore more effective at organizing power on an institutional basis within both church and society. Yet, since the 'conservative' wing typically lacks a prophetic critique of technologically oriented instrumental individualism, it tends to resist Catholic Social Teaching's sociological and ecological critiques of Liberal Capitalism.

---

[15] See again Robert Bellah *et al.* HABITS OF THE HEART.

In contrast, the late modern 'progressive' wing, while rejecting technologically oriented instrumental individualism, often lacks the skills of structural discipline and frequently fails to organize successfully on an institutional basis within both church and society. Further, because it is more sympathetic to the psycho-sexual dimension of expressive individualism, it often downplays bioethical issues like abortion, embryonic stem-cell research, and euthanasia, even while it remains strong in defense of the poor, peace, and ecology. As a result, although supporting the sociological and ecological critiques of Liberal Capitalism by Catholic Social Teaching, it often fails to engage with the concerns of Catholic Bio-Ethics.

Thus, while many Western Catholic lay movements appear to be counter-culturally prophetic, many nonetheless limit their counter-cultural critique to only one side or the other of late modern bourgeois breakdown. As a result, each one-sided partiality of the emerging postmodern lay Catholic wave carries a *residual late modern bourgeois limitation,* which is either 'conservative' or 'progressive.'

Yet again, as a result of these late modern bourgeois limitations, some followers of either strategy collapse into fear, resentment, and hatred toward the other side, rather than opening in loving dialogue to hope, compassion, and joy. Those who cultivate such polarization tragically abandon Jesus' Gospel of love. They block the Holy Spirit's postmodern call for prophetic-mystical regeneration of life's integral ecology.

Two Equal & Co-Creative Images
of the Divine Mystery

At the *deep mythic-symbolic level,* many late modern Western Catholic proponents of either the 'conservative' restoration strategy or the 'progressive' integration strategy sometimes seem tempted to celebrate only one side of what GENESIS 1:27 teaches us are the two equal images of the Divine Mystery.

The 'conservative' side of the current late modern Western societal and ecclesial polarization typically celebrates *the Classical Era's masculine transcendent symbols of the Divine Mystery*. But it typically forgets *the Primal Era's feminine immanent symbols of the Divine Mystery*, which still flourish within the profound consciousness of the Holy Spirit across the Eastern Orthodox and Eastern Catholic Churches. That 'conservative' one-sided strategy then often pursues one-sided and misguided psychological and sociological tactics.

- *Psychologically*, the 'conservative' side often holds up against Modernity's expressive individualism a reactionary attempt at resistance by retrieving *deformed hierarchical-patriarchal symbols* from classical European aristocratic culture. Indeed, the classical deformed-masculine aristocratic-patriarchal metaphor of "hierarchy" is still widely used as a name for the Catholic bishops. Yet we do not find that metaphor in the New Testament, since it expresses the reverse of Jesus's preaching about humble servant-leadership.

- *Sociologically*, the 'conservative' side often supports – again, contrary to Catholic Social Ethics – the modern materialist ideology of Liberal Capitalism, with its underlying *deformed hypermasculine symbols* from modern bourgeois culture. In so doing, the 'conservative side often rejects social-welfare functions for the state, despite Saint John XXIII's important declaration in MATER ET MAGISTRA that such examples of "socialization" are praised by Catholic Social Teaching.[16]

Both tactics – one psychological as well as classical and patriarchal-hierarchical, and the other sociological as well as modern and hypermasculine – draw on dysfunctional distortions of the masculine symbol-system.

---

[16] Recall also the prophetic teachings of the Hebrew Scriptures that the king should be the defender of orphans and widows. When the king abandons that role, he becomes idolatrous.

In addition, and in a distorted and even pathological masculine manner, some lay Catholic 'conservatives' within the United States have even embraced the destructive call for *constant warfare*, and for dramatic increases in funding for the national-security function of the state with its growing "military-industrial complex," all of which Catholic Social Teaching critiques. Such a call for constant military warfare represents a pathological spiritual deformation of the noble-warrior tradition.

Further, such 'conservative' calls are often joined with calls for constant "cultural warfare." That warring spirit then poisons the spirituality of its proponents with the hyper-masculine and culturally militarist infection of the late nineteenth-century Prussian *Kulturkampf* (meaning "culture-struggle").

Meanwhile, the 'progressive' side of the late modern Western societal-ecclesial polarization often creatively retrieves the Primal Era's feminine immanent image of God. By so doing, the 'progressive' side challenges the one-sided hegemony of the distorted and dysfunctional masculine symbol-system held up by many 'conservative' movements. Yet the 'progressive' side is often tempted to forget the deep-masculine symbol of the Divine Mystery as "Father."

Paradoxically, many on the 'progressive' side also often ignore or even reject the powerful Pentecostal movement still expanding across global Christianity. Yet currently, as the most dynamic global form of Christianity, Pentecostalism is spreading rapidly across planet Earth. Perhaps the reason for such dramatic growth is that the Pentecostal movement reveals at the deep-symbolic level the charismatic power of Holy Spirit as the feminine image of the Divine Mystery.

In addition and as mentioned, many on the 'progressive' side typically downplay importance for defense of the life of unborn humans, including embryonic human life, as well as defense of life for elderly and handicapped persons threatened by euthanasia. In so doing, they downplay Catholic Bio-Ethics. Similarly, many 'progressives' also appear to be unaware of the continuing bioethical threat of Eugenics, including from movements supporting bio-engineering of human nature (as with "Posthumanism" and "Transhumanism").

In contrast to these mirror-opposite partialities, this book proposes that the Holy Spirit is revealing the feminine symbolic face of the Divine Mystery, and is calling Catholics, as well as all Christians, and indeed the entire human family, to become open to the fullness of authentic postmodern spiritual energy. According to the vision proposed here, this spiritual energy celebrates *the egalitarian and co-creative partnership of the feminine and masculine symbols of the Divine Mystery.*

According to the vision of this book, the Holy Spirit is calling us to leave behind the classically aristocratic-patriarchal distortion of authority as elite male hierarchical domination. She is also calling us to leave behind the modern bourgeois hyper-masculine distortion of authority as elite male uprooting and fragmenting managerial manipulation. She is thus calling us to resist the spiritual deformation from both sides of the late modern societal-ecclesial polarization, and instead to synthesize the authentic spiritual gifts of both sides.

The deep solution to what Romano Guardini called "The End of the Modern World" cannot be simply to restore classical hierarchical-patriarchal discipline and order on the turbulent surface of late modern bourgeois society's integral-ecological degeneration. Neither can it be to continue to lose spiritual energy within the degenerative secularization and nihilization of late modern bourgeois Materialism.

Rather, holistic regeneration of the creative communion of the life's integral ecology requires re-awakening to the sacred character of the Cosmos, to the sacred character of our garden-planet Earth, to the sacred character of all of Earth's life, and especially to the sacred character of our human family's egalitarian and co-creative partnership between women and men.

Again, this book proposes that the Holy Spirit is calling postmodern Catholic lay movements, from both 'conservative' and 'progressive' sides, as well as "religious communities" and "clerical" bishops, presbyters, and deacons, to resist the late modern societal-ecclesial polarization. That polarization spreads the demonic infections of fear, resentment, and even hatred on both 'conservative' and 'progressive' sides. It undermines both the postmodern societal common good and postmodern ecclesial evangelization.

The ultimate loser in the late modern polarized divorce between Western Catholic Christianity's 'conservative' and 'progressive' wings is postmodern evangelization. A Church sinfully wounded by internal division cannot be credible as the carrier of regenerative healing to late modern polarized society. Its own festering and sinful wound of polarization blocks its regenerative communication of the Good News as healing and joyful love. Thus, the current 'conservative' versus 'progressive' polarization undermines the loving truth of Jesus' Gospel of life. That is why, at the Last Supper, Jesus prayed to the Father: "that they may be one in us, that the world may believe." (John 17:21b).

Let us hope and pray that postmodern ecological development of Catholic lay movements, along with postmodern ecological refounding of some Catholic "apostolic" communities, will lead to a co-creative partnership of solidarity seeking a regenerative conservative-progressive synthesis. Surely, the distinctly 'progressive' and 'conservative' emphases in spirituality need not be hostile opposites. Surely, there must be a creative path for their loving embrace in a fruitful life-generating manner.

Let us hope and pray that we will all hear the call of the Holy Spirit urging us to join together to seek regeneration for the evolving creative communion of life's integral ecology, throughout its inter-woven natural, human, and spiritual fabric, across our loving Crea-tor's beloved garden-planet Earth.

Awakening to
Postmodern Ecological Spirituality

As we are journey through the spiritual "Dark Night" of Modern In-dustrial Civilization, we are called to awaken to the Holy Spirit's lov-ing invitation to embrace Postmodern Ecological Spirituality. In that awakening, we are called to long prayerfully for the regenerative "Dawn" of Postmodern Ecological Civilization.

Again, as we have learned from recent discoveries in Science, our mystical Cosmos (and everything within it) is not simply being sus-tained. Rather, it is all still *evolving ecologically*. Hence, our emerging postmodern eco-spiritual consciousness realizes that our loving Cre-ator is still lovingly continuing to create our mystical Cosmos. Fur-ther, within our evolving and mystical Cosmos, all of our loving Cre-ators' beloved creatures are co-creatively contributing to the evolving cosmic expression of our loving Creator's Divine Creativity.

Wherever prayerful longing for global ecological regeneration arises, the living waters of Postmodern Ecological Spirituality are already beginning to flow, although so far only as a small and often unno-ticed stream, and not yet as a great flowing river. Even so, when we drink from *its life-giving waters,* we become prophetically and mysti-cally refreshed, so that we may seek regenerative pathways out of the late modern global degeneration of the sacred creative communion of life's integral ecology.

For that reason, this book urges both newer Catholic lay movements and older Catholic "religious" movements, as well as "clerical" dea-cons, presbyters, and bishops, and indeed the entire global Christian family, to listen prayerfully to the Holy Spirit's loving invitation to drink from the living and regenerative waters of the emerging Post-modern Ecological Spirituality.

Again, this means awakening – both mystically and prophetically – to our deep spiritual grounding in the sacred and still evolving co-creativity of the Cosmos, to our deep spiritual grounding in the sacred and still evolving co-creativity of Earth's planetary ecosystem, and to our sacred and still evolving grounding in our human family's co-creativity within Earth's biosphere.

Most importantly, in Christian form it means re-awakening – again, both mystically and prophetically – to the Sacred Trinity's loving co-creativity. That is the ultimate source and goal of the sacred creative communion of life's still evolving integral ecology within our sacred and still evolving mystical Cosmos.

In addition, through this awakening, mystical-prophetic streams within the late modern Western Christian Churches, both Protestant and Catholic, are now beginning to learn again from the rich and ancient Christian cosmic spiritual tradition that the Eastern Christian Churches, both Orthodox and Catholic, have constantly celebrated through songs of praise and thanksgiving to our loving Creator. Ancient Eastern Christian liturgies constantly and beautifully sing joyful songs of praise and thanksgiving in gratitude for the beauty and goodness of our loving Creator's beloved creation.

Again, this book proposes that the Holy Spirit is urgently inviting all Christian churches across planet Earth – Orthodox and Protestant and Catholic, East and West and North and South – to further develop the ancient Christian cosmic spiritual consciousness. In that development, we need to celebrate in prayerful and joyous song our still evolving and sacred cosmic creation as the *primary revelation* of the beauty, goodness, and truth of our loving Creator.

So full of goodness and beauty and truth is our loving Creator's sacred creation that ancient theologians like Saint Augustine of Hippo called the "*Book of Nature*" the first book of divine revelation. This first book of revelation needs to be read as the horizon and ground for our loving Creator's second book of revelation, which is of course the Bible.

Again, some mystical-prophetic individuals and communities within the Western Christian churches are already drinking deeply from the Holy Spirit's regenerative waters of the emerging Postmodern Ecological Spirituality. These individuals and communities are already awakening to the evolutionary creative communion of life's integral ecology, which is revealed throughout the co-creative evolution of our loving Creator's vast and majestic Cosmos.

Yet the Holy Spirit's Postmodern Ecological Spirituality has not yet found a comprehensive and integrated understanding within the Western Christian churches. So how can we help to develop such a profound mystical-prophetic consciousness, and (for this book's purposes) especially within Catholic Christianity? It is that question which the remaining chapters try to address.

4

REFOUNDING "RELIGIOUS LIFE" IN

ECOLOGICAL SPIRITUALITY

As new Catholic lay movements have emerged and grown, not only does the question arise of how will they further develop, but also the question of how older movements of "religious life," particularly modern "apostolic" forms, will relate to the new development. Will the new lay movements simply retreat into the sterile strategy of "restoration"? And will modern "apostolic religious movements" simple retreat to the margins of history with little hope for an influential future?

Or might both join hands in co-creative response to the late modern breakdown of the now globalized form of Modern Industrial-Colonial Civilization? Might both join hands to co-creatively seek the guidance of the Holy Spirit in nurturing the emerging seeds of Postmodern Ecological Spirituality and of a fresh Postmodern Ecological Civilization?

In response to these questions, I propose in this book that the Holy Spirit is calling both older and newer Catholic mystical-prophetic intentional communities, one lay and the other "religious," as well as the wider Catholic communion of Churches, the wider Christian family, and indeed our entire human family, to seek deep grounding in

Postmodern Ecological Spirituality. Further, in this book I propose that the Holy Spirit is calling us to do so in a way that synthesizes the prior authentic gifts of Christian and other human spiritualities.

Incomplete Late-Modern Transformation
of Lay & Religious Movements

The contemporary Western Catholic commitment to ecological ethics, and the beginnings of ecological spirituality, seem to be found more in the 'progressive' behavior of some "apostolic-religious" communities, especially some women's communities. In addition, seen, some women's "religious communities" have been creatively retrieving the Primal Era's *spirituality of feminine immanence*. As stated earlier, this ancient spirituality cherishes the feminine image of the Divine Mystery as announced in GENESIS 1:27.

By contrast, many emerging postmodern Catholic new lay movements on the 'conservative' side do not yet seem to have developed an ecological ethics or spirituality. Rather, many appear to cultivate only a human-oriented ethics and spirituality uprooted from ecology. Further, some in the still early wave of these new lay movements even defend the Classical Era's problematic aristocratic spirituality of defining transcendence as hierarchical and patriarchal.

As a result, it sometimes seems as if some 'conservative' sectors of the postmodern new lay movements, by virtue of their lay nature, are creating postmodern organizational structures, but are simultaneously attempting to restore classical clericalist spiritual consciousness. Meanwhile, it also sometimes seems as if some sectors in the 'progressive' "religious" communities are exploring postmodern ecological-spiritual consciousness, but simultaneously clinging to classical organizational "religious" structures. Perhaps this contrast is the Holy Spirit's way of provoking dialogue between new and old waves. Let us reflect further on this contrast.

Some "apostolic-religious" communities appear to be trying to become more relevant to the modern "secular" world. Yet this attempt paradoxically does not fully open their "religious" structures at an equal level to "secular" lay membership, which would include both sexes, singles and marrieds, and children. At the same time, with equal paradox, some new lay movements seem to be yearning nostalgically for a restoration of the authoritarian hierarchical-patriarchal values of the classical aristocratic male understanding of transcendence, even while they retrieve of the egalitarian lay identity of the original Jesus-movement.

In both cases, we have the double paradox of some "religious" 'progressives' clinging to a classically dualist organizational structure while pursuing holistic postmodern eco-spiritual consciousness, and some lay 'conservatives' creating a holistic postmodern organizational structure while restoring a classically dualist hierarchical-patriarchal consciousness.

Lurking somewhere in the future, there is hopefully a *co-creative 'conservative-progressive' synthesis* that will integrate postmodern holistic consciousness and postmodern holistic structures, and integrate the emerging Catholic Postmodern Ecological Spirituality with older Catholic spiritual traditions.

In response to the above paradox, I propose in this book that some modern "apostolic-religious" forms of Catholic mystical-prophetic intentional communities" consider linking with the postmodern lay spiritual energy. The birth of postmodern lay spiritual energy would thus provide the opportunity for an *ecological and lay-oriented refounding* by some modern "apostolic-religious" communities, if the Holy Spirit indeed is calling those communities to such a challenging path.

In a moment, we will reflect more on such refounding. But first let us look at three competing historical-strategic paths, as institutional choices available to modern "apostolic-religious" communities facing decline, and in some cases even death.

Three Competing Strategic Paths
for Apostolic-Religious Communities

Within the modern-to-postmodern transition, I propose that *three distinct strategic paths* are available to declining modern Western "apostolic religious" communities within 'advanced' industrial societies. Each of these three strategic paths is legitimate, and the choice of one or another belongs only to the communities themselves in their discernment of the Holy Spirit's call.

Path I
Survival by Premodern Restoration

Path I faithfully continues the original mission of the founder of a "religious" community, and it preserves certain cultural artifacts from its original style – for example, a "religious habit." While within the 'advanced' industrial world some of the "apostolic-religious" communities which follow that path may perish, others will survive and may even grow modestly by attracting new 'conservative' members.

Yet such surviving institutions will become less central in Catholicity's emerging postmodern lay ecological strategy. They will not provide transformative mystical-prophetic leadership for the emerging Postmodern Ecological Era. Even so, their spiritual gifts will remain important.

Again, the 'conservative' path will always remain a legitimate option that we need to cherish. The "apostolic-religious" communities which chose this path will play a secondary role in the future, just as coenobitical, monastic, and mendicant communities continued on a smaller scale beyond their age of historical dominance.

Path II
Ambiguity from Late Modern Integration

Path II positions itself ambiguously between premodern restoration and postmodern regeneration. It appears that this path of ambiguity is a common one for many "apostolic-religious" communities presently in decline within the 'advanced' industrial-center countries. Because this path appears so common, it may be helpful to reflect soon at some length on two dimensions of its ambiguity, with one on the external side of "apostolates" to the "secular world," and the other on the internal side of "religious" spirituality and structure. In a moment, we will examine this ambiguity in greater detail. But, first, let us identify the third path of refounding, which this book sees as the most fruitful one.

Path III
Refounding as Postmodern Regeneration

Path III explores a refounding alliance with, and partial embrace of, the postmodern lay ecological form and spirituality. In earlier stages of the tradition, some hermits became partial "monastics" ("cenobites"), as later some monastics became partial "mendicants," and still later as some mendicants became partial "apostolics." In such an alliance, some modern "apostolic" communities may embrace, at least partially, the new postmodern lay form and spirituality. Experiments in this embrace could become vital for the Western Church's postmodern regeneration.

Reflections on the Late-Modern Path
of Strategic Ambiguity

There are two sides to this ambiguity, one on the external side of "apostolates" to the "secular world," and the other on the internal side of "religious" spirituality and structure.

Integration of External "Religious Apostolates"
with Neoliberal Corporate Capitalism

First, there is the problem of ambiguity on the side of external "apos-tolates." One example of this occurs when some "religious communi-ties" sponsoring Catholic hospitals allow their hospitals to imitate for-profit secular hospitals in the neoliberal 'free-market' fantasy by blocking their own employees from organizing themselves into a democratic union.

When that happens, such "apostolates" accept the currently unjust model of the neoliberal corporate-capitalist healthcare system. Such unfortunate developments may be called the "neoliberal capitalist corporatization" of some late modern "religious apostolates" for health-care ministry. In such cases, their "apostolates" are *integrating with neoliberal secular modernization.* When that strategy is chosen, it is usually the result of the "religious" community having turned insti-tutional guidance for the "apostolate" over to presumably well-mean-ing lay trustees and administrators, who are often recruited from the leadership of 'Free-Market' capitalist corporations.

Such developments, however, can block the Holy Spirit from open-ing the prophetic imagination of sponsoring "apostolic-religious" communities to explore authentically postmodern co-creativity in healthcare. Authentic postmodern exploration in healthcare needs to be grounded in the emerging postmodern ecological paradigm of Cosmology for Philosophy and Science, as well as for management.

But that ecological paradigm is generally unknown to the presuma-bly well-meaning neoliberal corporate-capitalist elites typically serv-ing as trustees and administrators for Catholic healthcare institu-tions. Knowledge of the ecological paradigm is also not generally found within most members of the contemporary medical profes-sion, since the academic teaching of Biology still remains largely imprisoned within the modern cosmological paradigm of Scientific Materialism.

When some "religious communities" sponsoring Catholic healthcare "apostolates" pursue neoliberal corporate-capitalist integration, they probably will not attract young candidates who are searching for a postmodern ecological future. Nor will they probably attract young candidates who seek to preserve traditional values from the classical past. As a result, recruitment of new members for such "religious communities" will fail because of the late modern ambiguity.

A similar case occurs when some "religious communities" sponsoring Catholic universities allow their schools to become both organizationally and academically like late modern "secular" universities. These too are increasingly being "corporatized" by presumably well-meaning business-based trustees and administrators, who typically follow the late modern neoliberal capitalist model, and who often implicitly accept that ideology's underlying Cosmology of Scientific Materialism.

Despite having a chaplain, a chapel, and a Theology program, such Catholic universities can often fail to explore across all academic disciplines and in their institutional life the Holy Spirit's counter-cultural call to challenge the late modern bourgeois intellectual-spiritual degeneration of truth and wisdom, and the wider late modern bourgeois economic-technological devastation of life's integral ecology.

They can thus often collapse into the dysfunctional posture of so many late modern institutions operating within the now globalized late stage of Modern Industrial-Colonial Civilization. In that collapse, they can often allow – no doubt unconsciously, but nonetheless relentlessly – their non-theological curricula to teach the secularist, relativist, and sometimes even nihilist doctrines of the late modern Western intellectual-spiritual breakdown.

In addition, some Catholic schools, like their parallel Catholic healthcare institutions, often resist by managerial and legal means the desire of many of their employees to form themselves into a democratic union. Acting in the manipulative manner that Robert Bellah and his colleagues have called the "managerial ethos" of "instrumental individualism," those business-based trustees and senior managers can often in effect deny both the truth and the justice of the human right of employees to organize themselves into a democratic union.

Further, they can then frequently define such employee's unions as "outside third-parties," which denies that a union is a democratic organization of the employees themselves. They can in turn often hypocritically hire outside law-firms and management consultants (expensive "third parties") to lead them in an immoral battle against the truth and justice of the human rights of their own employees.

In both cases, one for healthcare and the other for education, some trustees and senior administrators of some Catholic institutions can sometimes cruelly reject Catholic Social Teaching's indisputable support for the human right of employees to form themselves into a democratic union.

Whenever they make such a rejection, such trustees and senior managers would commit *an objective social sin* against the regenerative inspiration of the Holy Spirit and against the life-giving Gospel of Jesus. When that happens, we might describe their tragic situation as the late modern "bourgeois captivity" of so many trustees and senior administrators of Catholic educational and healthcare "apostolates."

In such cases, by pursuing the integrating strategy of neoliberal corporate capitalist integration, such trustees and senior management of such universities can unconsciously block the Holy Spirit from opening their hearts and minds to explore regenerative postmodern co-creativity in healthcare and education.

Again, such a postmodern exploration would need to be grounded not in the dominant and degenerative intellectual legacy of Scientific Materialism, but rather in the regenerative vision of the Postmodern Ecological Cosmology and in the regenerative energy of Postmodern Ecological Spirituality.

Perpetuation of Internal
Spiritual-Structural Dualism

The other side of the late modern path of ambiguity for some "religious communities" is internal. It can often be found in the *dualistic spirituality* that typically undergirds the dualistic organizational structure. This second problematic of modernizing ambiguity can occur even though some "apostolic communities" try to become more "relevant" to Modernity by adopting "secular" dress, by being more active in "the world," and even by embracing postmodern ecological consciousness.

The ambiguity can arise because some "religious communities," despite trying to be externally relevant, do not transform their internal dualist spirituality, which is expressed in its internal dualist structure. That means that such "religious community" do not grow beyond Modern Psychological Spirituality, or beyond what may be called the institutional structure of a mono-sexual monopoly.

In so doing, such a community continues to exclude from core membership one sex, as well as married people and children. Again, in such cases the members are adopting 'progressive' consciousness, yet preserving 'conservative' spirituality and structure. They are thereby not opening themselves fully to the Holy Spirit's call to explore postmodern lay possibilities.

Again, the problem here can be that the path's mixed message impedes recruitment. Those who are attracted to the 'progressive' consciousness of the community's behavior may not be drawn to its 'conservative' structure. Those who are attracted to its 'conservative' structure may not be drawn to its 'progressive' consciousness. As a result, the path of ambiguity may lead to a community's decline, and for some even death. Yet, in the mystery of our loving Creator's Divine Providence, life-giving creativity arises even out of such a loss.

Ecological Refounding through
Islands of Regenerative Co-Creativity

Within the strategic framework of Path III, what might be the regenerative path of deep transformation for re-founding an "apostolic religious community" on Postmodern Ecological Spirituality and the postmodern lay ecological-spiritual model, while maintaining living roots in past traditions?

The New Zealand Marist priest and anthropologist Gerald Arbuckle has argued that re-founding requires embracing the myth of regeneration by entering into a *death-life cycle of transformation*. According to Arbuckle, this cycle follows three sequential stages.[1]

- *Foundation.* This is the original stage of *birth and growth,* flowing directly from the founder's original spiritual energy and with the founder's original vision, mission, and structure.

- *Crisis.* Later, there comes the stage of *decline and chaos,* which so many "apostolic-religious" communities have now experienced within 'advanced' industrial societies (beginning in the closing decades of the twentieth century). Institutionally, this represents for those institutions their spiritual "Dark Night." Yet this "Dark Night" can also become the dark womb of regenerative creativity. From within that dark womb, there can grow renewed life.

---

[1] See Gerald Arbuckle, STRATEGIES FOR GROWTH IN RELIGIOUS LIFE (Alba House, 1986). See also his OUT OF CHAOS: *Refounding Religious Congregations* (Paulist Press, 1988), and FROM CHAOS TO MISSION: REFOUNDING RELIGIOUS LIFE FORMATION (Liturgical Press, 1997)

- **Regeneration.** If there is *new birth*, then the community enters into regeneration, fed by a transformed vision, mission, and structure. Today, I have proposed, this means embracing the postmodern lay ecological form of spirituality and membership structure.

Yet regeneration requires *new founders*. The transformed vision, mission, and structure will not first come from committees or chapters. Rather, as Gerald Arbuckle and also Mary Jo Leddy have both proposed, it will first appear in visionary individuals.[2] If "religious communities" wish to pursue the path of postmodern transformation, they first need to discern the identity of their re-founding persons.

Communities pursing the path of postmodern regeneration could then support re-founding persons in what might be called "*islands of regenerative co-creativity.*" These could be small experiments in lay-centered ways of integral-ecological living as a postmodern Catholic mystical-prophetic community, outside the main structure of the traditional institutions yet in close dialogue with those institutions. Such islands of co-creativity would use cooperative capital and ecological technologies, and they would be guided by the egalitarian partnership of both feminine and masculine spiritual energies.

Such islands of regenerative co-creativity could gather women and men, singles and marrieds, and children as well, in *experimental ecovillages* for a return to ecological communion with our wounded Earth, to social communion with the marginalized poor, and to spiritual communion with the Divine Mystery as revealed in Nature.[3]

---

[2] See Mary Jo Leddy, REWEAVING RELIGIOUS LIFE: *Beyond the Liberal Model* (Twenty Third Publications, 1990).

[3] For more on ecovillages, see the next chapter. Such ecovillages, however, should not been conceived as stand-alone projects, but rather as experimental centers of postmodern ecological vision and spiritual energy humbly serving the regeneration of rural life in the surrounding bioregion. For more on this wider regional regeneration of rural life, see the brilliant and pioneering book by Anthony Flaccavento, BUILDING A

Further, these islands of regenerative co-creativity could ground themselves in natural, human, and spiritual ecology, in a spirit of extended family, and in a spirituality of the co-creativity of the feminine and masculine faces of the Divine Mystery. They could thus provide a life-bearing sacramental sign for regeneration of the sacred creative communion of life's integral ecology. These islands of regenerative co-creativity could seek to heal what Saint John Paul II called the "culture of death"[4]

Such islands of regenerative creativity could build bridges between their new experiments and the older community's traditional institutions – bridges of mutual sharing and dialogue. Over time, and as a result of dialogue between the two poles, traditional "religious" institutions could begin to be transformed into postmodern institutional forms serving regeneration of life's integral ecology.

Such transformed institutions could give witness to the regenerative power of the Holy Spirit and life-giving Gospel of Jesus for our wider society. They could show how we can all together regenerate the sacred and evolving creative communion of life throughout its interwoven natural, human, and spiritual fabric. Such transformed institutions could then become witnessing places where Earth is healed, where families are healed, and where the deep psychological wounds of the late modern individuals are healed – all in the warm embrace of the Holy Spirit.

In service of that mission, such postmodern islands of creativity could seek to become pioneering Catholic mystical-prophetic servants of the regeneration of life's evolving integral ecology. They could humbly seek to serve our loving Creator's beloved family of creatures, including our loving Creator's beloved human family.

HEALTHY ECONOMY FROM THE BOTTOM UP: *Harnessing Real-World Experience for Transformative Change* (University of Kentucky Press, 2016).

[4]Again, John Paul used this phrase in EVANGELIUM VITAE, Par. 12.

Ecological Revision of Vows
as Spiritual Promises of Regeneration

Let us now explore the question of how might the traditional "religious vows" of *poverty, chastity, and obedience* become regenerated for "religious communities" that chose to seek refounding through the lay transformation of Postmodern Ecological Spirituality?

As part of addressing this question, let us now in a lay style rename these "religious vows" as "spiritual promises." But then what might these spiritual promises mean? To answer this question, we need to be guided by the *deep spiritual mission* of regenerative postmodern mystical-prophetic communities. Once again, the proposed deep spiritual mission of postmodern global lay communities is as follows:

> *The Holy Spirit is now calling us, both personally and institutionally, to embody and to preach the Good News of Jesus in and through holistic regeneration of the evolving creative communion of life's integral ecology, throughout its interwoven natural, human, and spiritual fabric, across our loving Creator's beloved garden-planet Earth.*

That also implies helping to create a Postmodern Ecological Civilization, which will serve the regeneration of life's integral ecology at every level from the womb to the planet. In this way, such regenerative communities would provide a life-giving regenerative alternative to what Saint John Paul II called the late modern "culture of death."

Postmodern Spiritual Promise
of Poverty

In the postmodern lay ecological-spiritual refounding, the spiritual promise of poverty would not mean contempt for material creation, but rather the loving embrace of it. In this sense, poverty would mean owning few things, yet belonging in relationship to everything. In imitating the lilies of the field and the birds of the air, those making this promise would seek to become more consciously united with all of life on our garden-planet Earth.

This loving embrace would not be possessive, for the desire to expand controlling ownership has produced the *modern active-aggressive bourgeois-technological plundering of the material world*. That modern plundering is the mirror-opposite of the *classical passive-aggressive aristocratic-ascetical despising of the material world*. It is also the modern anti-ecological outcome of that classical anti-material despising.

Again, the classical aristocratic-ascetical contempt for matter and the modern bourgeois-technological addiction to its plunder are sequential anti-spiritual rejections of our loving Creator's self-revelation in and through the beauty and goodness of creation. The final result of modern consumerist Materialism is not love of matter, but rather its *integral-ecological devastation*.

Again, the loving embrace of material creation would be neither an act of contemptuous rejection nor one of possessive control. It would be a conscious expression of *loving communion* with all the species (including our human species) within our garden-planet Earth, and with the entire Cosmos. It would mean celebrating our rooted and relational participation in material creation, while being free of the desire to "subdue" it.[5]

Such a postmodern spiritual promise of poverty would be grounded in the theological affirmation that all material creation constitutes the

---

[5] The translation into English as "subdue" from the original Hebrew word in GENESIS 1:28, may be the result of subsequent patriarchal interpretations of early Hebrew narratives. One does not "subdue" a garden (Garden of Eden). Rather, one cares for it. See David K. Goodin, "Understanding Humankind's Role in Creation: Alternative Exegesis on the Hebrew Word *Kabash* and the Command to Subdue the Earth," STUDIES IN SCIENCE AND THEOLOGY, Vol. 10: STREAMS OF WISDOM? SCIENCE, THEOLOGY, AND CULTURAL DYNAMICS, ed. Hubert Meisinger, William B. Drees, and Zbigniew Liana (Lund, Sweden: Lund University Press, 2005), pp. 293-311.

"primary revelation," as Thomas Berry reminded us concerning the first and fundamental disclosure of the Divine Mystery in and through Nature.[6] Also and again, another and ancient way of expressing this truth is Saint Augustine's classical teaching that the "Book of Nature" is the first book of Divine revelation.

This postmodern spiritual promise of poverty rejects the classical spiritual *"fuga mundi"* (flight from the world). For this postmodern promise, material creation becomes the *foundational natural sacrament*, the first and fundamental expression of the Creator's loving *Logos* and *Eros*, revealed in the beauteous Cosmos of evolution's creative communion.

This postmodern spiritual promise of poverty would require a lifelong commitment to the regeneration of life's integral ecology, throughout its interwoven natural, human, and spiritual fabric, across our loving Creator's beloved garden-planet Earth. Those who make this commitment would also commit themselves to feeling deeply the pain of the late modern degeneration of life's integral ecology, and to feel it as spiritual pain.

In addition, they would promise to devote themselves, both personally and institutionally, to the regenerative healing of the deep ecological wounds increasingly inflicted on our loving Creator's beloved garden-planet Earth and on our loving Creator's beloved and myriad creatures of Earth, including our loving Creator's beloved human family.

This postmodern spiritual promise of poverty would also mean a lifelong commitment to the solidarity of human ecology with people who are poor, to defense of the special dignity human life at every

---

[6] See Thomas Berry & Mary Evelyn Tucker, THE SACRED UNIVERSE: *Earth, Spirituality, and Religion in the Twenty-first Century* (Columbia University Press, 2009).

stage, including not yet born humans, and to the struggle for justice and peace everywhere.

The promisors would try to live in close life-style and friendship with people who suffer from oppressive poverty – partly out of humble compassion, yet also out of the desire to learn from the profound traditional wisdom of many marginalized communities. Especially important for this commitment would be learning from *the rich wisdom-traditions of Indigenous Peoples*, many of who have remained close to our human family's ancient roots. For these peoples are living heirs to our human family's ancient and healing eco-spiritual resources.

In such transformed postmodern Catholic mystical-prophetic intentional communities, both single and married people would make the spiritual promise of poverty. In turn, the work of the members, many of whom would presumably be engaged in "secular" employment and not necessarily in church "ministries," could generate funds for the community.

Further, this promise, in terms of belonging to a particular community, could be for a lifetime or for a limited term, and so it would not be absolute. For such belonging is not a sacrament. As Jesus told his critics, the Creator made the Sabbath for humans, not humans for the Sabbath.

In sum, the postmodern promise of poverty would be a spiritual affirmation of the sacred and evolving integral-ecological life of our loving Creator's beloved creation. It would also be an act of spiritual solidarity with the regeneration of life's integral ecology, across our sacred garden-planet Earth, including the preferential option for the poor and in defense of the special dignity of human life at all stages.

Postmodern Spiritual Promise
of Chastity

While the traditional vow of chastity was frequently interpreted as the Platonic goal of escaping from our human body and our sexuality, the postmodern spiritual promise of chastity would be grounded in the sacred character of our body and of our sacred sexual energy of *Eros*. Further, this postmodern promise would counter the late modern trivialization of sexuality into a means of self-gratification within the commodity-fetish of the Liberal Capitalism's consumer society.

The modern consumerist trivialization of human sexuality is the active-aggressive counterpart to the classical Platonic passive-aggressive fantasy of escaping from the body. Thus, the postmodern spiritual promise of chastity would challenge in counter-cultural form both the modern reduction of sexuality to trivial self-gratification and the classically ascetical demeaning of sexuality as anti-spiritual. Instead, it would honor sexual energy as both deep and sacred, because it carries the regenerative energy of life. The postmodern spiritual promise of chastity would oblige its promisor to reverence sexuality's sacred depth and to channel its regenerative energy into life-giving paths.

This would mean honoring our sacred body as our first and fundamental participation in the natural sacrament of the sacred Cosmos. To be cared for through diet and exercise, our sacred body would then become our first and basic means of prayer, with that prayer expressed through word and gesture as well as in song and dance, and both individually and communally. For in our body, we have our deepest personal experience of God's loving self-manifestation through creation.

As the vast majority of the human race has always recognized, the basic life-giving channeling of our body's sexual energy occurs through the primal institution of family. Yet family is more than immediate spouses and children, for it embraces kinship across time and space, including both ancestors and those not yet born. Further, in its magnanimity it embraces friends through adoptive familial bonding, as in the Latin *compadrazco* relationship.

Ultimately, there are no final human boundaries to human families, except the human race itself. Further, our wider biological relationships include not only our human family with its rich diversity of cultures, but also all of our garden-planet Earth's other creatures, whom St. Francis of Assisi called his "sisters and brothers."

This diversity embraces the plants and animals who give up their organic lives as food for our human family, and who thus provide the constantly recycling material of our living human bodies. Similarly, the water that makes up so much of our bodies is billions of years old, and it remains a flowing part of the ancient yet continuing recycling of Earth's great hydrological cycle that includes clouds, oceans, rivers, and streams. Further, our extended kinship extends even to the Cosmos, for in the material of our bodies we find a gift from the carbon of exploded stars. Cosmos and Earth flow within us, and we with within Cosmos and Earth.

The spiritual promise of chastity would thus be a commitment to celebrate our bodily participation in our wider human family, in our wider family of all creatures within planet Earth, and in our vast cosmic family of creation. In addition, it would be a promise locally to help regenerative familial communities to grow, and globally to help to network these familial communities in support of the global regeneration of life's integral ecology.

Again, this postmodern spiritual promise of chastity would represent a Catholic mystical-prophetic witness against the modern trivialization of sexuality, as well as against the classical demeaning of it, by an authentically postmodern spirituality that celebrates the human body and human sexuality's co-creative life-giving energy as a profound expression of the co-creative life-giving energy of the entire Cosmos, and ultimately of its loving Creator.

Postmodern Spiritual Promise
of Obedience

Late modern bourgeois society propagandizes the consumer culture's expressive individualism, and as a result it often portrays obedience with a negative image. It tends to identify obedience with authoritarianism and repression. That is partly because in the Classical Era hierarchical-patriarchal male aristocratic elites often demanded unquestioning obedience and often exercised authoritarian control over subordinates. Modern emancipatory social movements rightly rebelled against that deformation of authentic obedience. One of greatest gifts of bourgeois Modernity has been to defend the individual person as carrying an inviolable integrity of freedom.

Yet bourgeois Modernity, following the Epicurean atomism of its cosmological foundation, wrongly defined the individual as *autonomous*, that is, as free from any bonds of obligation except those of legal contracts. Then, following the ultimately non-rational voluntarism of Epicurean Philosophy, Modernity wrongly defined human freedom as *arbitrary choice*, with no substantive or spiritual meaning.[7]

For those reasons, a recovery of meaningful obedience can become a healing step toward *postmodern communitarianism*, which honors the dignity and freedom of the human person, and also understands that the human person is nested within the wider ecological community of life, at once holistically natural, human, and spiritual.

In particular, modern Anglo-American legal theory and social theory have wrongly understood the individual as preceding community,

---

[7] It is perhaps not surprising that, in the movement promoting so-called "reproductive rights," the word "choice" (versus the word "life") becomes the core strategic theme.

with the community supposedly formed only by contracts of autonomous individuals. In fact, the opposite is true. The individual grows out of family and its wider community, and the individual remains an organic part of the integrally ecological community of life that is at once natural, human, and spiritual.

If, however, the human person indeed becomes atomized and uprooted, as the erroneous anthropological-cosmological paradigm of Modern Philosophy and Modern Science has wrongly imagined, the human person can experience great difficulty in the search for happiness and community. Again, it is not individuals who create community, but community that creates individuals. Individuals emerge in and through relationships, beginning with family relationships and expanding through friendships and wider networks of community.

The brilliant Catholic eco-philosopher Charlene Spretnak has persuasively argued that cultivation of relationship is an especially *feminine gift*. She has also argued that women's role in recovering relationality in all aspects of life needs to become a central part of healing the devastation of natural and social ecology by contemporary "ultra-modern" (and hyper-masculine) society.[8]

Again, the Classical Era laid an authoritarian and often repressive superstructure on the Primal Era's organic and egalitarian character of community, while the Modern Era rightfully rebelled against that repressive domination. From its emancipatory rebellion, Modernity then gave birth to the great wave of democracy that is still sweeping across planet Earth. Yet Modernity also began to uproot and fragment individual persons from the duties of legitimate communitarian obedience within the evolving creative communion of life's natural, human, and spiritual ecology.

---

[8] See again her pioneering book mentioned earlier, RELATIONAL REALITY.

Our postmodern task is to find regenerative integration for the rights of the human person with co-creative duties to communitarian solidarity. Regenerative obedience would seek integrating pathways that would simultaneously nurture personal integrity and communitarian solidarity. On the one hand, such pathways would avoid the Classical Era's authoritarian repression. On the other hand, they would avoid the Modern Era's uprooting fragmentation. Postmodern obedience as process would seek to synthesize person and community, while postmodern obedience as substance would seek to follow the call of holistic regeneration.

Within such a holistic communitarian style, the Catholic postmodern spiritual promise of obedience would find its deepest spiritual center in the promise to be obedient to the Holy Spirit's healing call for the regeneration of life's integral ecology, throughout its interwoven natural, human, and spiritual fabric, across our loving Creator's beloved garden-planet Earth.

5

CONCLUDING REFLECTION

At the end of this exploration, let us again recall the distinctive deep spiritual missions of the evolving waves of Catholic mystical-prophetic intentional communities from their past foundational, classical, and feudal waves, through to the now declining modern wave, and into the emerging postmodern wave. As we have seen, there are six historical long waves of these communities (counting the one now emerging), with each having a distinct historical mission.

- *Foundational Lay Communities.* The deep spiritual mission of the foundational early church, which was completely lay, was *to witness to the messianic message of Jesus,* largely from within the idolatrous, oppressive, and often persecuting Roman Empire.

- *Classical Coenobitic Communities.* The deep spiritual mission of the classical cenobites was *to keep alive the witness of the Cross of Jesus in their own spiritual martyrdom,* and to do so in prophetic counterpoint to the compromise with the Roman Empire by the hierarchical-patriarchal "clergy" of the urban Imperial Church. In addition, by befriending plants and animals, those cenobites tried *to live a prophetic life of eschatological return to an ecological Paradise,* like the biblical Garden of Eden.

- *Feudal Monastic Communities.* The deep spiritual mission of the feudal monastics – beginning with the great missionary project of the Irish-Keltic Monks and later taken over by Latin-Roman Benedictine monks allied with papal centralization – was, after the collapse of the Western Roman Empire, *to welcome, evangelize, and educate the migrating German tribes into the life-giving community of Jesus' disciples, and with their royal and aristocratic tribal leaders to regenerate Western Christian Civilization.*

- *Medieval Mendicant Communities.* The deep spiritual mission of the mendicants (again, meaning beggars) of the medieval bourgeois cities was evangelically to witness to the Gospel of Jesus by *challenging seminal bourgeois spiritual errors planted within medieval bourgeois culture by themselves living in poverty and embracing the poor, the natural world, human rights, education, and democracy.*

- *Modern Apostolic Communities.* The deep spiritual mission of "apostolic religious" communities of Modern Industrial Civilization was *to witness to the Gospel of Jesus by serving the new industrial working class, as well as immigrants, rural farming families, and colonized peoples, through modern social-welfare apostolates of health, education, and social welfare.*

- *Postmodern Lay Ecological Communities.* This book proposes that the fresh deep spiritual mission of emerging postmodern lay movements, and of "apostolic-religious communities exploring "refounding," is *to witness to the Gospel of Jesus by seeking holistic regeneration for the evolving creative communion of life's integral ecology, throughout its interwoven natural, human, and spiritual dimensions, across our loving Creator's beloved garden-planet Earth.*

The historical challenge faced by the new lay movements, and also refounding "apostolic-religious" communities, is the breakdown of the now globalized Modern Industrial Civilization and of its collapsing Modern Psychological Spirituality, with that breakdown and collapse revealed in the the growing global devastation of life's integral ecology.

In the vision of this book, emerging postmodern lay movements are called to ground their charisms, and what may be called their surface missions, in this deep spiritual mission for the great postmodern transition. This means deep seeking deep grounding in the emerging Postmodern Ecological Spirituality, and planting seeds for a Postmodern Ecological Civilization.

A special emphasis in this book has been the recent and sudden decline of the modern "apostolic" form of "religious life," and the parallel emergence and growth of the postmodern lay movements. Within that emphasis, the book has proposed a possible refounding of some "apostolic religious communities," or at least of some sectors that would function as "islands of co-creative regeneration." Again, such refounding would seek deep grounding in the emerging Postmodern Ecological Spirituality, and humbly work with others to seek a Postmodern Ecological Civilization.

This book has also proposed that growing postmodern lay movements and declining modern "apostolic-religious" communities cooperate with each other in an *eco-spiritual alliance* seeking to help regenerate rural life by planting *new lay ecological monasteries* in the form of *ecovillages,* and as humble focal points for regenerating rural life.

This book has called for that eco-spiritual alliance partly out of the fear that, if we lose the creative energy of so many declining "apostolic-religious" communities, and if the growing new lay movements do not drink deeply from the emerging Postmodern Ecological Spirituality, then the Western Catholic Church's evangelization will become weaker still, and may even become partly pathological – at least in the 'advanced' industrialized areas already experiencing the spiritual "Dark Night" of Modern Industrial Civilization.

118

Further, the book has proposed that, within the postmodern historical transition, the emerging fresh Catholic form of Postmodern Ecological Spirituality needs to synthesize the gifts of past forms of Catholic spiritual energy, as well as other human forms of spiritual energy. To that end, we need to pray to the Holy Spirit that she may
guide us beyond the increasingly anti-poor, anti-life, pro-war, and
anti-ecological breakdown of Modern Industrial Civilization.

In addition, the book has proposed that we need to ask the Holy
Spirit to guide us into regenerative, inclusive, and peaceful pathways
toward a Postmodern Ecological Civilization. Such a fresh civilization is called to seek the holistic regeneration of life's integral ecology,
and at every level from the human womb to our entire garden-planet.

If, however, the new Catholic lay movements develop without an
eco-spiritual alliance with their earlier "religious" predecessors, then
these new global lay movements could collapse into the 'conservative' cultural-spiritual temptation of late modern *restoration*. If that
were to happen, they would fail to give birth to the mystical-prophetic creativity necessary to seek globally authentic ecological, social, and spiritual *regeneration*.

Without such an eco-spiritual alliance, the important heritage of traditional "apostolic-religious" communities would presumably continue to decline, at least in the 'advanced' industrial regions. Then,
the Western Catholic evangelization would continue to weaken before the anti-spiritual triumph of the anti-poor, anti-life, pro-war, and
anti-ecological Modern Mechanical Cosmology of Scientific Materialism, and still worse of demonic Nietzschean Nihilism.

It is not this book's place to say which declining "apostolic-religious"
communities may be called by the Holy Spirit to seek transformation
through embracing the emerging lay-rooted Postmodern Ecological
Spirituality. Nor is it this book's place to say which growing new
postmodern lay movements should seek an eco-spiritual alliance

with the rich legacy of declining "apostolic-religious" communities, in order to promote the Peter Maurin's regenerative "Green Revolution."

Nonetheless, this book predicts that older modern "apostolic religious communities" and newer postmodern lay movements – if they chose to drink together from the living waters of the emerging Postmodern Ecological Spirituality – could together become co-creative partners in the local-global regeneration of life's integral ecology. Such co-creative partners could then become loving sources of healing for our global Christian family, for our wider global human family, and for the still wider and evolving creative communion of life across our loving Creator's beloved garden-planet Earth.

Thus far, however, the seeds of hope are few and scattered. So, we will conclude on a somber note by repeating the profound warning from Francis of Rome:

> *Doomsday predictions can no longer be met with irony or distain. We may well be leaving to coming generations debris, desolation, and filth. The pace of consumption, waste, and environmental change has so stretched the planet's capacity that our contemporary lifestyle, unsustainable as it is, can only precipitate catastrophes, such as those which even now periodically occur in different areas of the world. The effects of the present imbalance can only be reduced by our decisive action, here and now.*

LAUDATO SI'

ON CARE FOR OUR COMMON HOME

(Par. 161)

ACKNOWLEDGEMENTS

T his book has been developed in part from a background paper that I originally prepared a long time ago for the 1990 Annual Assembly of the U.S. Conference of Major Superiors of Men, held at Salve Regina College in Newport, Rhode Island. My gratitude goes to the Conference leaders at that time for the opportunity to develop the six-stage analysis of the historical long waves of these communities, as found in found in Chapter 2 of this book. I also did an expansion of that paper in 2009 and another in 2014.

For making that original paper and ultimately this book possible, I particularly thank Sister Pat Chaffee, O.P., Ph.D., a member of the Racine Dominican Sisters and a prophetic human-rights activist. During my years at the Center of Concern, Sister Pat Chaffee, with the support of her Racine Dominican community, did most helpful research on the history of "religious life." I would also like to thank Sister Rosaire Lucassen who, in her role then as the President of the Racine Dominicans, proposed that Sister Pat Chaffee volunteer at the Center of Concern.

A special thank-you goes also to Sister Ginny Sylvestri, a Sister of the American Province of the Servants of Mary, for inviting me, again many years ago, to do a video-program on that background paper. That experience helped to advance the analysis presented in this book.

More recently, I owe a debt of gratitude to Sister Maria Homberg and to Sister Peg Donovan, both members of the Maryknoll Sisters and sequential Directors of the Maryknoll Sisters Mission Institute, for inviting me to lead an Institute Seminar in 2014. That experience helped to bring closure to this book's development.

I would also like to thank an old friend from Ireland, John Sweeney, who first introduced me to the Irish-Keltic monastic tradition by bringing me to the ancient Irish-Keltic monastic site of Glendalough. That Irish-Keltic monastery, founded by Saint Kevin in the sixth century and nestled in a lush green valley within the gentle Wicklow Mountains, was once one of Ireland's great centers of learning for scholars from all across Europe. John also made it possible for me to visit Ireland many times as a guest lecturer, but in a situation where I was happily more learner than teacher.

Of course, none of the above good persons is responsible for any errors, limitations, or other problems found in this book. That responsibility is entirely my own.

 JOE" HOLLAND is an eco-philosopher and Catholic theologian exploring the global transition to Postmodern Ecological Civilization.

Joe completed his Ph.D. from the University of Chicago in the field of Ethics & Society, an interdisciplinary dialogue of Theology with Philosophy and Social Science. At Chicago, he studied Theology with David Tracy, Philosophy with Paul Ricoeur, and Social Science with Gibson Winter. He was also a Fulbright Scholar in Philosophy at the Universidad Católica in Santiago, Chile during the last year of the democratic-socialist government of Salvador Allende, which was overthrown by the murderous dictatorship of General Augusto Pinochet.

Joe is Emeritus Professor of Philosophy & Religion at Saint Thomas University in Miami Gardens, Florida and Adjunct Professor in its School of Law; Permanent Visiting Professor at the Universidad Nacional del Altiplano in Puno, Peru; President of Pax Romana / Catholic Movement for Intellectual & Cultural Affairs - USA and Editor of its Pacem in Terris Press, with both based in Washington DC; Vice-Chair of Catholic Scholars for Worker Justice, with offices in in Boston, Massachusetts and at Georgetown University in Washington DC; and a member of the International Association for Catholic Social Thought, based at the Catholic University of Leuven in Belgium.

Earlier, Joe served for 15 years as Research Associate at the Washington DC Center of Concern, created jointly by the international Jesuits and the US Catholic Bishops to work with the United Nations on global issues. Later, he taught at New York Theological Seminary in New York City, at the Theological School of Drew University in Madison, New Jersey, and at the Florida Center for Theological Studies in Miami, Florida. For both the Center of Concern and Pax Romana, he served as NGO Representative to the Economic and Social Council of the United Nations in New York City.

Joe also served as Research Coordinator for the 1976 Theology in the Americas Conference. In addition, he co-founded the American Catholic Lay Network, the National Conference on Religion & Labor (co-sponsored by the AFL-CIO), and Catholic Scholars for Worker Justice. Plus, he was founding Director of the Pallottine Institute for Lay Leadership & Research at Seton Hall University.

Joe has published 15 other books and many articles. His book with Peter Henriot, *Social Analysis: Linking Faith and Justice*, has more than 100,000 copies in print, including 2 US editions, 5 foreign-language editions, and 2 foreign English editions. He was also writer for the 1975 document *This Land is Home to Me* (A Pastoral Letter on Powerlessness in Appalachia by the Catholic Bishops of the Region), and for its 1995 sequel document *At Home in the Web of Life* (A Pastoral Message from the Catholic Bishops of Appalachia on Sustainable Communities).

In the United States, Joe has lectured at Georgetown, Harvard, Notre Dame, Princeton, and many other universities. Internationally, he has lectured at Institut Catholique in Paris, France; Sophia University in Tokyo, Japan; Pontifical Catholic University in São Paulo, Brazil; Pontifical Catholic University in Porto Alegre, Brazil; Universidad Mayor de San Andres in La Paz, Bolivia; and Universidad Nacional del Altiplano in Puno, Peru.

In 1986, Joe received the Boston Paulist Center's Isaac Hecker Award for Social Justice; in 2002, the Athena Medal of Excellence from the Universidad Nacional del Altiplano in Puno, Peru; and in 2013 the Irish Echo's Labor Award for contribution to the US labor movement. Joe is married to Paquita Biascoechea Holland, a native of Puerto Rico, and they have two wonderful grown children and four wonderful young grandchildren. His too infrequent hobby is sailing, especially in the beautiful green waters of the Caribbean Sea.

APPENDIX

PACEM IN TERRIS
ECOLOGICAL DECLARATION

A humble and prayerful encouragement, at the end of the Modern World,
for ecologically concerned Christians and other concerned spiritual seekers
to advance the Postmodern Ecological Renaissance,
which we believe the Holy Spirit is calling forth
within our loving Creator's beloved human family
across our loving Creator's beloved garden-planet Earth.

Revision of 1 September 2016
World Day of Prayer for the Care of Creation

A Working Paper issued by
PACEM IN TERRIS ECOLOGICAL INITIATIVE
which is the core project of
PAX ROMANA / CMICA-USA
1025 Connecticut Avenue NW, Suite 1000, Washington DC 20036 USA
www.paceminterris.net | office@paceminterris.net

When you send forth your spirit, they are created,
and you renew the face of the Earth.

Psalm 104: 30

T his Declaration, issued by the Pacem in Terris Ecological Initiative and serving as its guide, is included at the end of this book because Pacem in Terris Press (which has published this book) is part of the Initiative. Still in development, the Initiative is a project of Pax Romana / Catholic Movement for Intellectual Affairs - USA (CMICA-USA), which is based in Washington DC. The Initiative includes this Declaration, Pacem in Terris Press, and Pacem in Terris Ecovillages Project.

This Declaration promotes what it calls the "Postmodern Ecological Renaissance." Looking beyond the "End of the Modern World," this Renaissance seeks holistic regeneration for the evolving creative communion of life's integral ecology, throughout its interwoven natural, human, and spiritual fabric, across our loving Creator's beloved garden-planet Earth.

In the Initiative's name, the phrase "Pacem in Terris" (Peace on Earth) is taken from the title of the famous 1963 encyclical letter by Saint John XXIII on world peace. The phrase "The End of the Modern World" is taken from the title of the ground-breaking 1950 book by the late and distinguished Italian-German and Catholic philosopher, Romano Guardini.

Within the Declaration, the phrase "integral ecology" is taken from the great papal encyclical letter LAUDATO SI', issued in 2015 by Pope Francis. "Integral ecology" connects natural ecology with human ecology, since human ecology is nested within the wider system of natural ecology and remains part of it. In addition, integral ecology is supported by ecological spirituality, which is also described here as mystical-prophetic "spiritual ecology."

To mark the inauguration of the Pacem in Terris Ecological Initiative, this Declaration was first issued on 19 January 2012 by Pax Romana / CMICA-USA as a Working Paper under the name of the "Washington Declaration." This current version, still a Working Paper and now re-named the "Pacem in Terris Ecological Declaration," is dated 1 September 2016, which was the World Day of Prayer for the Care of Creation.

We live today amidst the global integral-ecological breakdown of
MODERN INDUSTRIAL CIVILIZATION.
Within late modern neoliberal globalization,
that breakdown is now devastating life's integral ecology,
throughout its evolving and interwoven natural, human, and spiritual fabric,
across our loving Creator's beloved garden-planet Earth.

Despite Modernity's important and abiding contributions,
its late modern global ecological devastation
is the outcome of deeply anti-ecological errors,
embedded within Western Modernity's philosophical-scientific Cosmology,
and within Western Modernity's deeper symbolic-mythic foundations.

WESTERN MODERNITY'S PHILOSOPHICAL-SCIENTIFIC COSMOLOGY
has wrongly imagined that humans are not organically part of Nature.
In turn, it has wrongly imagined that Nature itself is not organic,
but rather atomistic, mechanical, and materialist,
and thus has no spiritual meaning.

WESTERN MODERNITY'S SYMBOLIC-MYTHIC FOUNDATIONS,
lodged at a deeper level of human consciousness than Cosmology,
have wrongly imagined that modernization should be guided
primarily by a pathological hyper-masculine and anti-feminine degradation
of the ancient archetype of the noble warrior.

Because of Western Modernity's materialist Cosmology
and because of its deformed masculine and anti-feminine symbolic-mythic foundations,
modernizing elites across the globe have wrongly imagined
that they should conquer and exploit Nature without limit,
that that should constantly pursue economic, political, and even cultural warfare,
and that they should conquer, exploit, marginalize, and even eliminate certain humans,
as if all were only utilitarian commodities without spiritual meaning,
and available for individualistic utilitarian manipulation.

Those modern Western cosmological and symbolic-mythic errors
have in turn misguided Modernity's two dominant ideologies of Materialism,
which we know as "Liberal Capitalism" and "Scientific Socialism."
Despite their abiding and complementary societal insights,
those materialistic ideologies have erroneously misdirected late modern societies
into the global devastation of life's integral ecology.

In the now acute stage of late modern global ecological devastation,
democratic liberal states promoting late modern neoliberal globalization
have entered into economic alliance with dictatorial communist states.
Both have been jointly supporting an anti-ecological global industrial system
that has unleashed ancient and demonic idolatries of
money, power, exploitation, inequality, and violence.
Those idolatries are being unconsciously promoted across planet Earth
by late modern neoliberal networks of
global financial institutions, global cultural industries,
and even globalized universities.

To heal the contemporary global devastation of life's integral ecology,
we believe that the Holy Spirit is now calling all of us across
our loving Creator's beloved human family
to undertake the turbulent, confusing, and dangerous journey beyond
MODERN INDUSTRIAL CIVILIZATION,
since it has now become globally destructive of integral ecology,
and spiritually bankrupt.

To assist with this historic global journey,
we also believe that the Holy Spirit is inspiring
eco-spiritual leaders across our global human family
to plant humble seeds for global regeneration of life's integral ecology.

We further believe that the Holy Spirit is calling our entire human family
to develop those seeds of regeneration into an emerging
POSTMODERN ECOLOGICAL CIVILIZATION,
which needs to be nourished by the vast and deep ecological wisdom
of our human family's rich and diverse spiritual traditions.

To help in planting seeds for global regeneration of life's integral ecology,
we humbly and prayerfully encourage
our concerned Catholic, Orthodox, and Protestant sisters and brothers,
including members of all twenty-four "sui juris" Catholic Churches,
as well as all concerned spiritual seekers,
to promote what we call the emerging
POSTMODERN ECOLOGICAL RENAISSANCE.

As humble and prayerful disciples seeking
to follow the loving and life-giving Way of Jesus,
we rejoice that visionary Christian individuals and movements,
across our loving Creator's beloved human family,
as well as other visionary and concerned spiritual seekers,
are already advancing this Renaissance.

To further advance this Renaissance,
we encourage concerned Christians and other concerned spiritual seekers,
across our loving Creator's beloved garden-planet Earth,
to gather in small eco-spiritual communities
for prayer, study, and dialogue,
and there to read what Jesus called the "Signs of the Times,"
and to employ the "See-Judge-Act" method of praxis.

To support the task of study by these eco-spiritual communities,
Pax Romana / CMICA-USA offers the humble services of this still developing
PACEM IN TERRIS ECOLOGICAL INITIATIVE.
The Initiative recommends that these small eco-spiritual communities
undertake a long-term study of the following intellectual-spiritual resources
for postmodern global regeneration of life's integral ecology:

First,
OUR HUMAN FAMILY'S ECOLOGICAL WISDOM TRADITIONS,
including the traditional ecological wisdom of indigenous peoples,
the traditional ecological wisdom of world religions and philosophies,
the traditional ecological wisdom of rural communities,
and the traditional ecological wisdom of women;

Second,

THE BIBLICAL SPIRITUALITY OF CREATION,

which, according to Eastern Christian traditions,
proclaims that we humans are "priests of creation,"
called to care for our loving Creator's beloved human family,
and for our loving Creator's beloved family of all creatures,
and to do so with constant and joyful prayers of praise and thanksgiving;

Third,

THE BOOK OF NATURE & THE BOOK OF THE BIBLE,

which, according to ancient Eastern and Western Christian traditions,
constitute the two complementary books of Divine revelation,
with the first read though eyes of art, reason, and science,
and the second read though eyes of liturgy, faith, and theology,
and with both revealing our loving Creator of the Cosmos;

Fourth,

POSTMODERN GLOBAL CHRISTIAN ECOLOGICAL TEACHING,

including the ecological teachings of the Eastern Churches,
particularly the ecological messages of
the Greek Orthodox "Green Patriarch" Bartholomew I,
along with ecological statements from the World Council of Churches,
and ecological statements by national Protestant denominations,
as well as Catholic papal and national ecological statements,
and especially Pope Francis' great ecological encyclical LAUDATO SI';

Fifth,

THE POSTMODERN PHILOSOPHICAL-SCIENTIFIC "NEW COSMOLOGY,"

which goes beyond Modernity's atomistic, mechanical, and materialist "Old Cosmology,"
which celebrates a co-creative and (for some) a mystical understanding of evolution,
and which for postmodern eco-spiritual Christians find its Alpha and Omega
in the endlessly overflowing and co-creative love of the Holy Trinity.

Most importantly,
we humbly and prayerfully encourage eco-spiritual communities
to ask the Holy Spirit to guide all of us in planting seeds
for regenerating the evolving creative communion of life's integral ecology,
throughout its interwoven natural, human, and spiritual fabric,

130

across our loving Creator's beloved garden-planet Earth.

We also ask for constant prayer that the Holy Spirit guide our
PACEM IN TERRIS ECOLOGICAL INITIATIVE,
so that it may humbly and prayerfully help to advance the emerging
POSTMODERN ECOLOGICAL RENAISSANCE,
and so that it may humbly and prayerfully encourage more concerned Christians,
as well as more concerned seekers from other spiritual traditions
to plant postmodern seeds for the global regeneration of life's integral ecology.

We have published this Declaration
in hope that concerned Christians and other concerned spiritual seekers
will become inspired to search for visionary and co-creative paths
for the postmodern global regeneration of life's integral ecology.

We have also published this Declaration
for the sake of our children and our children's children,
and for the sake of the present and future children of all living creatures
across our loving Creator's beauteous but threatened Biosphere.

We humbly and prayerfully dedicate this Declaration
to Africa's late great feminine ecological leader from Kenya,
WANGARI MAATHAI,
and to the Native-American Nature-mystic and Lilly of the Mohawks,
SAINT KATERI TEKAWITHA,
as well as to
ALL ECO-SPIRITUAL YOUNG WOMEN AND YOUNG MEN,
who are working to plant seeds of regeneration
for the evolving creative communion of life's integral ecology,
throughout its interwoven natural, human, and spiritual fabric,
across our loving Creator's beloved and beauteous garden-planet Earth.

Let us constantly pray that together we may help to bring forth
a regenerative postmodern integral-ecological future
for our global Christian family,
for our global human family,
and for our global family of all creatures,
across our loving Creator's beauteous and beloved
garden-planet Earth.

OTHER BOOKS FROM
PACEM IN TERRIS PRESS

AFRICANA STUDIES

DJUANKAYU

THE BASSA-AFRICAN CREATION STORY
A Postcolonial Practical Theology
Pianapue T. K. Early.

AFRICAN ENCOUNTER OF FAITH & CULTURE
Ritual & Symbol for Young People
in Tiv Society of Central Nigeria
Clement Terseer Iorliam, 2020

BOTTOM ELEPHANTS
Catholic Sexual Ethics & Pastoral Practice in Africa:
The Challenge of Women Living within Patriarchy
& Threatened by HIV-Positive Husbands
Daniel Ude Asue, 2014

HUMANITY'S AFRICAN ROOTS
Remembering the Ancestors' Wisdom
Joe Holland, 2012

CHRISITAN SOCIAL TEACHING STUDIES

SUMMARY & COMMENTARY FOR PACEM IN TERRIS
The Famous Encyclical Letter
of Pope John XXIII on World Peace
Joe Holland, 2020

CATHOLIC LABOR PRIESTS
Five Giants in the United States Catholic Bishops Social Action Department
Volume I of US Labor Priests During the 20th Century
Patrick Sullivan, 2014

CATHOLIC SOCIAL TEACHING & UNIONS
IN CATHOLIC PRIMARY & SECONDARY SCHOOLS
The Clash between Theory & Practice within the United States
Walter "Bob" Baker, 2014

PACEM IN TERRIS
Its Continuing Relevance for the Twenty-First Century
(Papers from the 50th Anniversary Conference at the United Nations)
Josef Klee & Francis Dubois, Editors, 2013

100 YEARS OF CATHOLIC SOCIAL TEACHING
DEFENDING WORKERS & THEIR UNIONS
Summaries & Commentaries for Five Landmark Papal Encyclicals
Joe Holland, 2012

THE "POISONED SPRING" OF ECONOMIC LIBERTARIANISM
Menger, Mises, Hayek, Rothbard: A Critique from
Catholic Social Teaching of the Austrian School of Economics
Pax Romana / Cmica-usa
Angus Sibley, 2011

BEYOND THE DEATH PENALTY
The Development in Catholic Social Teaching
Florida Council of Catholic Scholarship
D. Michael McCarron & Joe Holland, Editors, 2007

CHRISTIAN STUDIES

ROMAN CATHOLIC CLERICALISM
Three Historical Stages in the Legislation of a Non-Evangelical,
Now Dysfunctional, and Sometimes Pathological Institution
Joe Holland, 2018

CATHOLIC PRACTICAL THEOLOGY
A Genealogy of the Methodological Turn to Praxis,
Historical Reality, & the Preferential Option for the Poor
Bob Pennington, 2018

SAINT JOHN OF THE CROSS
His Prophetic Mysticism in the Historical Context
of Sixteenth-Century Spain
Cristóbal Serrán-Pagán y Fuentes, 2018

POSTMODERN ECOLOGICAL SPIRITUALITY
Catholic-Christian Hope for the Dawn of a Postmodern Ecological Civilization Rising
from within the Spiritual Dark Night of Modern Industrial Civilization
Joe Holland, 2017

PADRE MIGUEL
A Memoir of My Catholic Missionary Experience in Bolivia
amidst Postcolonial Transformation of Church and State
Michael J. Gillgannon, 2018

WORLD RELIGIONS, ECOLOGY, & COSMOLOGY STUDIES

A Himalayan Hope

AND A HIMALAYAN PROMISE
India's Spiritual Vision of the Origin, Journey,
& Destination of Earth's Environment & Humanity
Thomas Pliske, 2019

THE WHOLE STORY:
The Wedding of Science & Religion
Norman Carroll, 2018

LIGHT, TRUTH, & NATURE
Practical Reflections on Vedic Wisdom & Heart-Centered Meditation
In Seeking a Spiritual Basis for Nature, Science, Evolution, & Ourselves
Thomas Pliske, 2017

THOMAS BERRY IN ITALY
Reflections on Spirituality & Sustainability
Elisabeth M. Ferrero, Editor, 2016

SPIRITUAL PATHS TO
A GLOBAL & ECOLOGICAL CIVILIZATION
Reading the Signs of the Times with Buddhists, Christians, & Muslims
John Raymaker & Gerald Grudzen, with Joe Holland, 2013

THE NEW DIALOGUE OF CIVILIZATIONS
A Contribution from Pax Romana
International Catholic Movement for Intellectual & Cultural Affairs
Pax Romana / Cmica-usa
Roza Pati & Joe Holland, Editors, 2002

Other Books By Joe Holland

In Addition to books published by Pacem in Terris Press

MODERN CATHOLIC SOCIAL TEACHING 1740-1958
The Popes Confront the Industrial Age
Paulist Press, 2003

"THE EARTH CHARTER"
A Study Book of Reflection for Action
Co-Author Elisabeth Ferrero
Redwoods Press, 2002
(also Italian & Portuguese versions)

VARIETIES OF POSTMODERN THEOLOGY
Co-Editors David Griffin & William Beardslee,
State University of New York Press, 1989

CREATIVE COMMUNION
Toward a Spirituality of Work
Paulist Press, 1989

AMERICAN AND CATHOLIC
The New Debate
Co-Editor Anne Barsanti
Pillar Books, 1988

VOCATION AND MISSION OF THE LAITY
Co-Author Robert Maxwell
Pillar Books, 1986

SOCIAL ANALYSIS
Linking Faith and Justice
Co-Author Peter J. Henriot SJ
Orbis Books, 1980 & 1983
(also versions in many languages)

THE AMERICAN JOURNEY
A Theology in the Americas Working Paper
IDOC, 1976

This book and other books from Pacem in Terris Press
are available at:

www.amazon.com/books